Dave is the best in the world at combining judo and jiu-jitsu. I wish I could get him to come teach at my school.
   —**BJ Penn, Brazilian Jiu-Jitsu World Champion, UFC World Champion**

Dave is like the Michael Jordan of BJJ, and he could very well be pound for pound the best BJJ player in the world. In my experience I often find that great athletes can't be great teachers, but Dave has the ability to teach a monkey how to armbar. . .He has added the final touches to a world-class fight gym. He has helped train world-class fighters and taken them to new levels! He's given AKA a whole new look on training BJJ. . . Dave as my instructor is the best thing that could ever happen to my UFC career. He has helped me grow as a fighter and has opened my eyes. . .My career will only grow even more as I continue working with him.
   —**Josh Koscheck, UFC Fighter**

Dave Camarillo is one of the few instructors I've met who not only has a wealth of knowledge in jiu-jitsu, but also the ability to convey it in easy-to-understand terms.
   —**Forrest Griffin, UFC Fighter**

Dave's jiu-jitsu has given me the confidence to use my stand-up to its fullest potential. I am no longer worried about getting taken down. If the fight goes to the ground, I feel that my opponent could be in even more trouble!
   —**Mike Swick, UFC Fighter**

Who is the most complete takedown/submission coach in the business? Just remember the six C's. Clear, Confident, Concise, Clarity, Competence=Camarillo!
   —**Mike Van Arsdale, UFC Fighter**

Dave is a master grappler with an aggressive submission oriented style. He is not only talented himself, but he is a great instructor who has helped transform our fighters' ground game.
   —**'Crazy' Bob Cook, MMA Fighter and Trainer**

Once I started the introduction, I couldn't put it down. Guerrilla Jiu-Jitsu beautifully weaves together Dave's judo experience, his jiu-jitsu experience, his political philosophy, and his new, integrated grappling system. This isn't just a cutting-edge instructional book; it's also the fascinating story of the birth of a new art and the development of the mind that produced it.
   —**Barry Eisler, author of *Killing Rain***

Books by Erich Krauss

Mastering the Rubber Guard with Eddie Bravo

Muay Thai Unleashed with Glen Cordoza

Beyond the Lion's Den with Ken Shamrock

Jiu-Jitsu Unleashed with Eddie Bravo

Brawl: A Behind-the-Scenes-Look at Mixed Martial Arts Competition with Bret Aita

Little Evil: One Ultimate Fighter's Rise to the Top with Jens Pulver

Warriors of the Ultimate Fighting Championship

Wall of Flame: The Heroic Battle to Save Southern California

Wave of Destruction: The History of Four Families and History's Deadliest Tsunami

On the Line: Inside the US Border Patrol

GUERRILLA JIU-JITSU

Revolutionizing Brazilian Jiu-Jitsu

Dave Camarillo with Erich Krauss

Victory Belt Publishing

California

www.VICTORYBELT.com

First Published in 2006 by Victory Belt Publishing.

(ISBN 13) 978-0-9777315-8-9
(ISBN 10) 0-9777315-8-8

This book is for educational purposes. The publisher and authors of this instructional book are not responsible in any manner whatsoever for any adverse effects arising directly or indirectly as a result of the information provided in this book. If not practiced safely and with caution, martial arts can be dangerous to you and to others. It is important to consult with a professional martial arts instructor before beginning training. It is also very important to consult with a physician prior to training due to the intense and strenuous nature of the techniques in this book.

Printed in Hong Kong

CONTENTS

2 FROM THROWS TO SUBMISSIONS

3 FLYING ATTACKS

ACKNOWLEDGMENTS

A very special thanks goes out to my parents, Jim and Linda, for giving me everything I needed to get where I am today. Without my father's constant pursuit to make me the best martial artist possible, I would have a completely different perception of what it means to be dedicated. And without my mother's quest to keep my life balanced, I would have cracked a long time ago.

Despite our different philosophies, I am forever grateful to Ralph Gracie for his direct contribution to the art, my training, and my life!

To my brother, for showing me the true meaning of talent, training with me all those years, making me tough as a youngster by beating the hell out of me, and for being incredibly selfless when it came to putting this project together.

A warm thanks for my wife, Shumei, for making the negative aspects of my life more positive, keeping me in line, and aiding me in seeing how to reach my full potential. Without her, I would still be living in a warehouse down by the river.

To Ernest "Waffle" Ellender for his guidance in everyday life, giving me the necessary strategies to handle frustration, and being such a genuine friend.

If it weren't for the guys on the San Jose State Judo Team, I would be half the man I am today. Man, you guys are tough! That is especially true with Dave Williams, a guy who has put so much effort in at SJSU and always believed in me, even when I was an arrogant jiu-jitsu practitioner. And a big thanks to Shawn Williams (hollywoodbjj.com) for being one of the nicest guys in jiu-jitsu and helping me with my game.

I owe so much to the Imamura family for taking care of me all those years and throwing me at will. I'm also indebted to Paul Schreiner, a man I consider to be my instructor.

I have to thank Josh Resnick for standing by me for so many years and teaching my students world-class judo! And I've got to thank Benjamin Ross for making me laugh and keeping me on my toes with his genius wit.

I'd like to thank everyone at the 131st Para-Rescue Squadron at Moffett Field, especially TSgt Mike Malloy. In addition to being a wonderful friend, he has helped me when I was down and taught me great life lessons through his military stories, which have increased my understanding of those in the US Military. They're the bravest souls on the planet.

A massive thanks goes out to the folks at On The Mat, particularly Scott Nelson and Gumby Marquez. They have been great friends and instrumental to my career. I'd also like to thank everyone at Dave Camarillo.com, particularly Joe Corrano.

I can't say enough about Greg and Lauren Glassman, the developers of Cross Fit. I would also like to thank Mike Zuegar from Ameritec Capital in Los Gatos, Howard Liu of HCK Kimonos (who has helped and supported me as a friend for years), my good friend Fumi Ishi from Forte Media, and Dennis Chinchek from Sportswear.

Last but not least, I would like to thank all my students and training partners. To my students in Minnesota, including Damian Hirtz, Jared Feierbend, and Brock Larson, you guys rule! To everyone at AKA, including Javier Mendez, 'Crazy' Bob Cook, and the AKA fighters, you guys are the toughest martial artists on the planet. And to my good friend BJ Penn—I know you've heard this before, but you're a phenomenon.

ABOUT THIS BOOK

After dedicating my entire adolescence to the sport of judo, I picked up Brazilian Jiu-Jitsu at the age of nineteen to get a little variety. Spending hours everyday in different gyms in an effort to excel at both, I had the unique opportunity to compare the two disciplines and discern their strengths and weaknesses. With my background, it didn't take long to realize that judo had a lot more to offer as far as throws and grip fighting. The fast and aggressive nature of the sport also develops important attributes such as speed, strength, and timing. However, training in the new discipline made me realize how superior jiu-jitsu was in the groundwork department. While judo players use their strength and speed to hunt for submissions on the mat, jiu-jitsu players use finesse, which requires a tremendous amount of technique. Once I had earned a black belt in both judo and Gracie Jiu-Jitsu, it seemed only natural to combine the aggression with the finesse, the grip fighting with the submissions, and the throws with the groundwork to create a more complete system. The result was Guerrilla Jiu-Jitsu.

As the head jiu-jitsu instructor at the world-renowned American Kickboxing Academy, I passed my system onto Josh Thomson, Mike Swick, Mike Van Arsdale, Paul Buentello, Jon Fitch, Trevor Prangley, and Josh Koscheck, and they used that system to reap havoc in their bouts in the Ultimate Fighting Championship. I passed Guerrilla Jiu-Jitsu onto my group of tournament competitors, and when I took twenty of them to the US Open, they completely dominated. While their opponents tried to rack up points on the judges' scorecards, my students combined the best elements from two highly effective styles and continuously went after submissions. At the end of the night ten of my guys brought home gold medals, and most of the others brought home either a silver or bronze.

Unlike many jiu-jitsu instructors, I do not teach my students to win tournaments by points. Guerrilla Jiu-Jitsu is geared toward winning tournaments by forcing your opponent to tap. If you are looking for a book that will teach you how to gain small points in competition and then stall your way to victory, this book is not for you. But if you are searching for an aggressive style that is revolutionizing traditional jiu-jitsu, then I suggest that you read on.

The book is broken down into three sections. The first section opens with basic judo skills. Once you feel comfortable getting your grips, chucking your opponent, and taking falls, the section then applies the throws and other judo techniques you acquired to your jiu-jitsu game. It explains how to force an opponent in a low jiu-jitsu stance into a higher stance so you can toss him through the air. It gives you alternatives for stopping wrestling shots. The section even describes how to throw an opponent who drops to one knee to avoid your newfound stand-up skills.

The second section builds off the first. It begins by describing what I call the Impact Control Position, which is the most dominant and effective position to assume after throwing your opponent. Off the Impact Control Position, the sections lays out dozens of submissions that you can easily transition into without getting caught in your opponent's guard. It also describes ways to establish side control when your opponent jumps guard and a half dozen other techniques that you will find invaluable in competition and training.

The last section of the book covers flying attacks, something you will not find in any other book. You might ask yourself why you would want to learn flying attacks. After all, seldom do you see them used effectively in competition. Well, the reason you never see them in competition is because few people do them right. Over the course of ten years, I refined the flying attacks already in existence. I created a dozen more. During my competitive career in Europe, Asia, South America, and the United States, I became infamous for my flying attacks. I defeated dozens of the world's best judo players and jiu-jitsu practitioners by jumping into the air, crashing a leg down on their neck, and assuming the triangle position five feet off the ground. Before my body came down onto the mat, my opponents were already tapping. I submitted so many people with flying attacks at an A-level judo event in Italy that I heard they were trying to ban them. A friend of mine jokingly calling it the 'Dave Camarillo Rule.'

After passing my flying attacks onto my students, they are now submitting opponents left and right with flying omoplatas, flying triangles, and flying armlocks. A few of my students are becoming so dangerous with their flying attacks their opponents jump guard the second they draw close. If you learn and hone just a few of the flying techniques I have laid out in this book, you will have an edge on virtually every competitor out there, whether he is a judoka, a jiu-jitsu practitioner, or an MMA fighter.

I've designed this book to be read and studied from start to finish. It is not just a bunch of random moves, rather a system that will significantly improve your jiu-jitsu game by combining the strengths of judo with the strengths of jiu-jitsu. With an arsenal of throws at your disposal, as well as a stealthy ground game, you will be able to take your opponent out of his comfort zone and dominate the fight. Although jiu-jitsu is one of the most effective martial arts on the planet, it has weaknesses just like everything else. I created Guerrilla Jiu-Jitsu and this book to plug those holes.

THE BIRTH OF GUERRILLA JIU-JITSU

When I walked into Ralph Gracie's Brazilian Jiu-Jitsu Academy back in January of '96, I strapped on a brand new white belt. Although I had no prior jiu-jitsu training, I ended up tapping a number of his advanced students that first day on the mat. Ten practices later, I received my blue belt. I've been around the sport nearly a decade now, and rarely have I heard of someone receiving a blue belt in less than a year. And never have I heard of someone earning one in just ten practices. It wasn't that I possessed superior strength or had submissions somehow ingrained in my DNA. The reason I excelled so quickly at jiu-jitsu was because I had been training judo day in and day out since the age of five.

In my opinion, judo is by far the toughest martial art out there. It is brutal, radical, and fast. Some of my earliest memories are training in the dead of winter, getting chucked so hard on old Tatami mats that I swear I felt my spirit leave my body. I remember bloodstains on my gi and fingers so tattered and torn I could hardly hold a pencil in class. My father was determined that my brother Dan and I would become Olympians, and as a result judo became our family religion. The byproduct was that I earned my black belt at the age of sixteen from Sensei Imamura, the head instructor at Fresno State University and my father's longtime coach.

My confidence got yet another boost when I spent my first summer in a Japanese dojo at the age of seventeen. A decade of practicing five hours a day had given me speed, strength, and timing. It had also given me a keen understanding of body movement. I remember submitting a fellow classmate with an armlock while in Japan, and then watching the head coach punch the kid as hard as he could in the chest for getting beat by an American. Rather than feeling guilt, I felt a sense of pride. From that moment on, I picked my training up a notch. I wanted the whole class to get socked in the chest. As far as I was concerned, I was going to rule the planet with judo.

Tearing up the competition circuit in the United States while still in my teens, including winning the high school nationals, I was pretty certain that I was nearing my full potential. Then I suffered a knee injury and was forced to focus exclusively on groundwork. At about the same time, I saw Royce Gracie work his magic in the first Ultimate Fighting Championship, submitting his opponents with this art called Brazilian Jiu-Jitsu. Then I saw Ralph Gracie compete in some MMA tournaments. I didn't think their art was superior to judo in any way, but I thought it looked pretty cool. I was living in Fresno, California at the time, and after doing some research, I learned that Ralph had a school in Pleasant Hill just a couple hours away. I asked my father if he would pay for a few months of tuition, and instantly he said no. It was the same as when I was in high school and wanted to play football. As far as my father was concerned, if it wasn't judo, then it was a waste of time. Still determined, I gathered up some Christmas money I had received, and then sneaked over to Pleasant Hill one afternoon.

Ralph and Cesar Gracie owned the academy at the time, and when they saw me tapping out their blue belts that first day, they realized that I had potential in the sport. I'm not saying that I was more technical than the guys I went up against, because I wasn't. As far as groundwork, jiu-jitsu is far more technical than judo. What allowed me to run through practitioners who had been training jiu-jitsu for two or three years was the attributes I had garnered from judo. Trying to throw an opponent who doesn't want to be thrown is not easy. You have to learn how to grip fight. You have to learn how to move your legs. Unlike slowly hunting for positioning and submissions in jiu-jitsu, everything is fast and explosive in judo, and you have to be in excellent shape to excel. So I already had a massive leg up on my jiu-jitsu opponents who were used to grappling with other jiu-jitsu practitioners. They just couldn't match my speed, strength, and timing. They were far more technical, but my attributes overpowered their technique. I even did some stand-up with Ralph that first day and tossed him around. Once we hit the ground I was in serious trouble, but I knew submissions would come easy because of my understanding of body movement.

Ralph and Cesar pulled me aside and started giving me private lessons. Ten practices later I had my blue belt. Now at that point I had a difficult decision to make. My main focus was still judo.

I had an offer to live at the Olympic Training Center in Colorado and eat and train for free. It was a tremendous opportunity, especially because I still had the goal of competing in the Olympics. I understood that the only way to reach a world-class level in the sport was to eat, breathe, and sleep judo. That is exactly what I would have been doing, but I turned the offer down. I had dug my fingers just deep enough into jiu-jitsu to realize that it might have something more to offer me. If I could combine the speed, strength, and aggression of judo with the technical groundwork of jiu-jitsu, I would be more complete than the majority of judo players out there. I would be a danger both on my feet and on the ground, which in my mind was a winning combination.

To be able to do both I moved to the Bay Area. I enrolled in San Jose State University, which had one of the best judo teams in the country. They had won the Collegiate Nationals something like thirty-four out of thirty-six times, so I knew in the judo department I would be just fine. Ralph Gracie had also opened up his own academy in Mountain View, which was less than a minute walk from where I was living. So I started doing judo full time, jiu-jitsu full time, going to school full time, and working a full time job. My goal was to reach my full potential in both sports, making sleep unimportant. It turned out to be a rough couple of years, but the advancements I made in my game far exceeded any of my expectations. Unfortunately negatives came along with the positives.

Because of the technical groundwork I acquired through my jiu-jitsu training, I started tapping out my fellow teammates at judo practice. They didn't like the funky submissions I pulled out of my arsenal, and neither did the coaches. This was particularly true with one of the head coaches,

Dave Camarillo surrounded by his world-renowned students at AKA

a 255-pound mountain of muscle who I nicknamed Bruiser. As a member of the World Team and a strict judo player, he thought there was no room in his discipline for jiu-jitsu. I don't know if it was because of his ego or if he feared something new, but he regarded jiu-jitsu as insignificant. One of the other head coaches, a rough man who I nicknamed Bully because he purposely tried to give his students cauliflower ears, understood Bruiser's disdain for my innovations. He decided to fuel the conflict.

One day Bruiser was spouting off about how jiu-jitsu had nothing to offer. He claimed all jiu-jitsu practitioners were weak and scrawny.

"Then why don't you go with Dave?" Bully said. "He's got a hundred pounds less than you, but I'll bet he'll tap you out."

"You actually want to bet on that?" Bruiser asked.

"Sure I want to bet."

"How much?"

"Fifty bucks."

"OK, your on," Bruiser said, and then he turned to me. "When do you want to do this, Dave?"

"Anytime, anywhere," I said, thrilled at the chance to finally shut Bruiser up.

"All right, then how about the next time we practice."

"You're on."

Well, it was off-season for judo and I was spending most of my time down at Ralph's. I didn't see Bruiser for a while, and then I started hearing through the grapevine that he was telling everyone I didn't have heart because I wasn't showing up at judo practice. It would do no good to tell him that I was trying to better my game by focusing on jiu-jitsu, so I called him up and told him to meet me down at the jiu-jitsu academy. He arrived after I had trained intensively for an hour. Bruiser threw on his gi and warmed up. I put an ice pack on my back in an attempt to recuperate some strength.

"So what are the rules?" Bruiser asked Ralph.

"You can't punch," Ralph said. "But other than that, there are no rules."

"So if he gets me in an armlock, I can slam him?"

The thought of a 255-pound man slamming me on my head wasn't appealing, and instantly I interjected. "We don't do that."

Ralph shook his head at me. "No, that's fine. You can slam him on his head if you want."

Bruiser smiled, and I walked over to Ralph to see why he had said such a thing. Was he trying to kill me? His answer was simple: If we play by his rules and beat him, then we really win.

So Bruiser and I went at it. In less than twenty seconds, I had his arm. I didn't want to injure my coach, so I didn't put much pressure into the lock. I thought he would admit defeat and tap, but instead he picked me up and started walking toward the door. In that moment I knew exactly what was going on in Bruiser's mind. He was going to walk outside onto the concrete and then slam me on my head.

Ralph jumped in front of the door, and I realized I had to finish Bruiser right then and there. Still dangling from his arm, I laid into the submission and popped his elbow. As he dropped, I climbed to my feet. My anger and frustration from his challenge rushed through me and I landed a quick kick to his head. I told him that he wasn't welcome in the jiu-jitsu academy anymore. He ended up sitting in his car for more than an hour, during which time a number of scenarios played out in my head. This included the possibility of him coming back in and going postal on us. I was comforted by the fact that the academy had a back door.

I thought that would be the end of my conflict at San Jose State, but then I got into it with

Bully, the coach who had instigated the challenge between Bruiser and me. One day we were practicing groundwork and I was tapping him right and left. I'd catch him in a choke, then an armbar, and then another choke. Every time I tapped him, I would roll away so he could recover. Instead of waiting for me to roll back toward him, he jumped on me when my back was turned. I would escape, and then submit him again. When the bell finally rang, he was pissed.

"We're going again!" he shouted.

"I don't want to," I said, and then bowed respectably.

"I don't think you heard me. We're going again."

"No. You're acting crazy, jumping on my back like a mad man."

"We're going again!"

"What is your problem?" I asked. "I tapped you out in front of everyone and you can't handle it?"

"Either we go again or you get out of here!"

I couldn't believe that this was coming from a coach and I left. It wasn't until later that I realized I was partially to blame for these repeated negative encounters. I had developed a lot of confidence with my new abilities, but when mixed with my immaturity, it often came across as arrogance.

Despite the flack I received, I continued on my mission undaunted. Having just received my purple belt in Brazilian Jiu-Jitsu, I felt I had reached a high enough level in both sports to combine their strengths into a system. The logical place to start was from the standing position because both judo and jiu-jitsu matches begin on the feet. Jiu-jitsu mainly focuses on groundwork, and it doesn't have much to offer in the takedown department. Judo, on the other hand, is primarily a standing art. Naturally, I would use judo techniques such as throws and foot sweeps to get my opponent to the ground. But in order to land in such a way that I could control my opponent and transition to jiu-jitsu ground techniques, I couldn't haphazardly throw my opponent. If I just threw my opponent without thinking about how I would finish him, he would have a chance to escape my potentially dominant position and turn the tide of battle. That is when I realized that submissions do not start once the fight goes to the ground; they start from the standing position. More specifically, they start the moment you grip your opponent.

A whole new world suddenly opened. When I established my grips on an opponent, I would not only use those grips to throw, but also use them to control my opponent when we hit the ground. Out of this came what I call the 'Impact Control Position.' It is a position that can be easily and quickly attained after every throw, and because you keep your original grips, you give your opponent less opportunity to escape. To get even more in-depth, I developed a host of submissions that you can effortlessly transition into from the Impact Control Position.

As I was working on all of that, I also started playing around with flying attacks. I had seen a guy catch one of Frank Shamrock's fighters with a flying armbar in a fight, and then I was further exposed to them when I attended a seminar being given by Oleg Taktarov, a Russian sambo master who had fought in the UFC in the early days. After breaking them down, I realized that people rarely landed flying attacks in competition because they were trying to assume the standard armlock position while in mid-air, which could be easily countered. Instead of jumping into the standard armlock position, I started jumping up into a triangle position. It was just like jumping guard, except I would jump a little higher. I'd smash my leg down between my opponent's shoulder and neck, which would rattle him and allow me to transition into an armlock. Soon I had developed more than a dozen flying attacks based on the triangle position.

Armed with my new system, I started wrecking shop at judo competitions. In '99 I won the Canadian Open. Later that year, I placed fifth at the Korean Open, which was an A-Level event. Then in 2000 I took my fire to the Italian Grand Prix and had the best performance of my life. None of my matches went the distance. I choked a Russian unconscious, I had huge throws, and I submitted two of my opponents with flying armlocks. Combining the two disciplines seemed to be working flawlessly. Every time I squared off with a guy, I didn't look at him as an excellent judo player. I saw him as a white belt in jiu-jitsu, and I treated him as such.

In my last match at the Italian Grand Prix, I was up against an excellent judoka from Wales for the bronze medal. A few minutes into the match, I was losing on small scores because I was hunting for submissions rather than trying to win on points. So I set this guy up and armlocked him hard. I could hear tendons popping. His first reaction was to lift me off the mat to get a restart. But as he lifted me up, he was tapping because of the pain. The referee called 'mate', I let go, and my opponent remained on the mat, cupping his mangled arm. When he finally got up and we squared off again, his whole game changed. He grabbed his collar with the hand of his mangled arm because there wasn't much he could do with it. He extended his good arm and started pushing me away, trying to keep me at bay. He was still ahead on points, and if he could run down the clock, he'd get the victory. Instead of letting him get away with that, I flew up and took his extended arm. At that point, flying armlocks were as natural for me as getting up in the morning. Because he got out of my last armlock by lifting me off the mat, I went to break his arm. By the time we hit the ground, he was screaming and the match was over. I saw the guy the next week at a competition in Holland, and in order to compete he had taken cortisone shots in both elbows.

A few days after I left Italy, a group of officials got together to discuss Dave Camarillo and his crazy flying armlocks. They thought they were downright dangerous, and they wanted to ban them. If I had been there for these meetings, I would have told them that flying attacks are a whole lot less dangerous than most judo techniques. Every time you throw an opponent, you could potentially drop him on his shoulder and end his career, which had actually happened to a contestant in Italy. You could even drop him on his head and end his life. I was just attacking the elbow. The flying armlock is quick, and it can hurt, but my opponents simply had to tap to get out of them. In my opinion, the meetings were held because they felt threatened by something new. They wanted to get rid of flying attacks because they didn't understand them. I suppose I should have felt bad in some way about the 'Dave Camarillo Rule', but I actually felt proud. I was bringing something to judo that people wanted to end.

There was also plenty of positive feedback. Dave Long, a high-level referee, told me how much he admired my ability to jump into the air and land with my opponent tapping. And when competing in Canada, the head coach for the British team mentioned that I had great newaza, meaning ground skills. It struck a cord with me because he said it several times and then stood there as if he was searching for something more to say, but he just couldn't muster the words. When combined with the admiration I received from my fellow teammates over my flying attacks, I decided that I was truly onto something. I decided to do more flying attacks than ever.

Later that year I was fighting RJ Cowen, a top-level 73-kilo player, for third place at the Senior Nationals and I caught him in a flying armlock. He was saved by the stand-up rule as he was tapping, but the damage had already been done to his elbow. His father was a high-level coach, and he came running across the mat, yelling at me. The referees got together to discuss whether or not I should be penalized, but they couldn't get away with it because I didn't actually apply the submission while in the air. I had just set the submission up for when I hit the ground.

My system worked just as well in jiu-jitsu competitions. As a blue belt I had ten matches, and I tapped every single one of my opponents. As a purple belt, I began by entering a tournament in LA. After dominating my weight division and catching one guy in a flying armlock, I entered the absolute division. I went up against Garth Taylor, who went on to win the world's down in Brazil later that year. I thought he was going to absolutely crush me with his hundred extra pounds, but I ended up throwing him twice because I had judo integrated into my jiu-jitsu game. Later that year I fought Fredson Paxiao, who is now a world champion black belt. He was undefeated at the time, the match was on his home turf in Brazil, and I was a heavy underdog. I took the fight on two days notice, yet I defeated him on points.

I maintained my strategy and went on to win half a dozen high level jiu-jitsu competitions, including the Joe Moreira International. Every time I engaged an opponent on my feet, I would instantly gain control of the match because I understood how to grip fight. I'd chuck my opponent to the mat, assume the impact control position, and then use my original grips to transition to a submission. I quickly developed a reputation for big throws and flying attacks, and pretty soon every time I stepped forward, my opponent would instantly jump guard.

Continuing to hone my skills, it started looking more and more like my dream of reaching the Olympics might materialize. But then things started to head downhill. The way you earn Olympic points is by medalling in the big tournaments, and the majority of big tournaments were in Europe. I had kicked butt in Italy, the Senior Nationals, Canada, and a host of other tournaments. I was ranked number two in the United States at the time. But because I was spending most of my time training, I couldn't make enough at my job to pay for a bunch of plane tickets overseas. I was waiting for grant money to come in, but that grant money never showed up. Jimmy Pedro was ranked number one at the time, and he got all sorts of grant money to travel the globe on the competition circuit. While

Dave Camarillo and BJ Penn at the K-1 Tournament in Honolulu, just hours before Penn defeated Renzo Gracie.

I had spent the last of my savings to compete in a few competitions abroad and rack up thirteen points, he had competed in dozens of competitions and racked up more than thirty points. He was arguably the best judo player to ever come out of the United States, and even though he had beaten me in the 1999 Senior Nationals, in which I took third place, I felt I could do much better if I got another shot at him. The Olympic trials would have been a perfect opportunity to do that, but at the time it just so happened that no Olympic trials were being held.

While I was trying to figure out how to raise the money to attend more judo competitions, I started getting discouraged with the training I received at San Jose State. It seemed as though the coaches were not willing to put in the effort needed for our team to excel and win. They were also very closed-minded. There were frequent meetings where the coaches would ask the team what we thought they could do to make the program better, and at each of these meetings I would raise my hand and say that I wanted to teach jiu-jitsu and focus more on the technical side of groundwork. I knew that it would help the team, and my competitive record was proof. I was consistently pulling off moves that no one had ever seen before. And none of my opponents or training partners could touch me on the ground. In my mind the team and the coaches only had something to gain, but every year they ignored my desire to teach jiu-jitsu to the team. After years raising my hand and getting turned down, I realized that creating the best team possible was not on the coaches' agenda.

I started looking at training elsewhere, but it didn't take long to realize other judo coaches had the same narrow outlook. The moment you mentioned the word jiu-jitsu, they instantly shut down. In their minds, jiu-jitsu had nothing to offer them, and they used all their energy to convince their students of this. They acted as if I were trying to destroy the constitution rather than just amend it to fit with the times. Whether they liked it or not, jiu-jitsu had forever changed the grappling arts, but instead of integrating some new techniques into their wonderful discipline, they would much rather get left behind. After dedicating my life to judo, I found it discouraging to say the least. The lack of support began to effect my motivation, and that is when I think I abandoned my plans of one day going to the Olympics.

Things weren't going much better over at the Gracie Academy. Since day one Ralph had been a very good, but rough, instructor. In the early years I hadn't thought much about his style of teaching, but after receiving my black belt and being more exposed to the martial arts community, I realized that I didn't always agree with his methods. For example, one afternoon back when I was a blue belt, I was at the academy with BJ Penn and a few other guys. Ralph walked in, and I headed over to him to give him a big hug. Instead of hugging me back, he threw me to the ground and jumped on top of me. I thought that he wanted to grapple, and then he started punching me in the face with closed fists. For fifteen minutes he beat on me with everything but the kitchen sink. By the time

I crawled to my knees, I had a broken nose and blood streaming down my face. At the time I rationalized his actions. I told myself that Ralph had roughed me over because he wanted to see what kind of student he had and to ensure that his team was tough, which it was. It wouldn't have been so bad if those were actually his intentions, but that surely didn't seem to be the case.

In my opinion, Ralph would have got much more out of his students if he had allowed us to prove ourselves through our determination. He could have helped us reach our full potential by taking our advice and treating us with respect.

Realizing that I would never mesh well with his methods, I approached Ralph one afternoon when I was a brown belt to tell him that I was finished. He pulled me into a little room with Batata, one of his black belt instructors, and then locked the door behind us. It was unnerving to say the least, but I stuck to my guns and told them that I was done. Ralph's retort was straightforward.

"If I ever catch you teaching jiu-jitsu, I will hurt you."

At the time I thought he might actually be able to stop me from teaching jiu-jitsu. I had dedicated my life to the sport, and the thought of being banned from teaching others on the mat hit me hard. I also desperately wanted my black belt. I should have seen the red flags, but at the time I wasn't yet confident enough to part ways. I ended up falling right back under his control, which is exactly where he wanted me. In the back recesses of my mind, however, I started searching for a way out.

After finally earning my black belt in February 2003, I heard from my friend Alex Khanbabian that there was a position open for the head jiu-jitsu instructor at the American Kickboxing Academy in

San Jose. AKA had been home to Frank Shamrock for a number of years, and the gym had graduated dozens of top-level MMA fighters and grapplers. I got an interview with Javier Mendez, the world champion kickboxer who owned the Academy. He knew that I had trained under Ralph Gracie, but I told him that I didn't want to open my school under the Gracie name. If I did, I would be restricted to what and how I taught. As a matter of fact, only about thirty percent of what I taught would come from Ralph. I had changed many of the techniques he taught me because I felt there were more efficient ways of applying them, and then I had added all kinds of new approaches to positions and submissions. I would also integrate judo into the program to create the most well-rounded group of jiu-jitsu practitioners out there. If all went well, we would be cleaning up at the competitions in no time.

After breaking down my plans for Javier, telling him about how I wanted to constantly get feedback from my students to create an open-minded atmosphere, he told me that he liked what he heard. Two days later, I was instructing fifteen jiu-jitsu practitioners who had gone without a coach for two weeks.

I had no plans to be involved with the professional fighters at AKA, but at the time Josh Thomson was training for his upcoming fight with Gerald Strebendt in the UFC. A UFC camera crew had come to the gym for the day, and they wanted to capture some of his moves on film. Josh asked me if I wanted to roll, so I instantly stripped off my gi and climbed onto the mats. Ten minutes later, I had caught him in half a dozen submissions. The following week I was made one of the head MMA coaches and started training the fighters.

In addition to this, I had also been teaching at a jiu-jitsu Academy in Modesto on Saturday mornings for a number of years. The owner had gotten into a bad motorcycle accident, and my brother and I had stepped in to help him out. While keeping his academy afloat, we created a group of well-rounded jiu-jitsu players. Even though the pay was minimal, I was extremely proud of our accomplishments there.

Things were falling into place as far as teaching, which meant that I spent less and less time at Ralph's. Then one day I found out over the internet that Crosley Gracie, Ralph's cousin, had been kicked out of the academy. Crosley had been a friend of mine for five years, so I wanted to give him a call to see what happened. I asked my roommate, who also trained at Ralph's, if he could get me his number. My roommate asked Batata, and Batata told Ralph. A couple of days later I got a call from Ralph while warming my guys up at AKA.

"Why are you trying to get ahold of Crosley?" he wanted to know.

"Because he is a friend of mine, and I just want to find out what is going on."

Then Ralph tore into me, and I replied by saying OK a dozen times and telling him how sorry I was, even thought I didn't know what I was apologizing for. Despite my subservient attitude, Ralph picked it up a notch and started with the intimidation.

"You want to find out what is going on, you call me, mother fucker," he said. "If you go behind my back again, it will be ruins for you. You understand that?"

I told him that I understood, but when I hung up the phone my entire time under his domination hit me like a ton of bricks. In less than ten seconds, I decided that I would never again train with Ralph Gracie. I would never speak to him again. I was finished with coaches trying to limit what I learned so they could own me. Having finally developed the confidence to be on my own, I would never go back to an environment where everyone put blind faith into the instructor.

After publicly announcing my split, a massive weight lifted off my shoulders. I felt my jiu-jitsu career could only get carried upward, but then one afternoon I got a call from one of my students in the Modesto Academy. He told me that Ralph planned to show up and teach my Saturday class. I had put six years into training those guys, and I considered many of them my close friends. I wasn't going to just abandon my class, so the following Saturday, understanding the unpredictable nature of the situation, I rounded up a bunch of the UFC fighters from AKA, including Josh Thomson, Josh Koscheck, and John Fitch, and we all headed down to the academy in Modesto. Instead of finding Ralph, I discovered one of his black belts ready to teach. I ended up teaching the class, but I had a strong feeling that it would be for the last time. I talked with the owner after practice, and I could tell Ralph was putting him in a tight spot. He said he was still trying to make his mind up as to which one of us he would go with, but I already knew that Ralph's tactics had succeeded. I had been bumped out of the picture.

It was a rough blow, but it allowed me to put more focus into my guys at AKA. I did everything opposite to the way I learned. I constantly got feedback from my students on how I could make the program better, and then I bent over backwards to implement their suggestions. Although most of my students came to learn jiu-jitsu, I started a weekly judo class to add rolls, grip fighting,

throws, flying attacks, and other judo techniques to their repertoire. As I watched my students excel at a phenomenally fast rate, I grew even more frustrated with all the instructors who believed that controlling knowledge and their students is the best way to run an academy. That attitude had been imbedded in the eastern martial arts long before the first UFC, and the Brazilians had maintained that philosophy when they introduced jiu-jitsu. And that attitude was spreading like wildfire. I remember going to Japan to do a seminar, and it was advertised everywhere as being open to the general public. But when I arrived, the only students attending were from the academy where the seminar was held. The place was packed, but there wasn't a single student from an outside academy. So the attitude that 'You only learn what I have to teach you' had even reached the Japanese jiu-jitsu scene.

In my opinion, narrow-minded instructors and their antidemocratic ideas had no room in such a wonderful sport. Whether they were Brazilian or American, I wanted to put every last one of them out of business. The way I tried to achieve that was by creating the most respectful students possible and having them dominate at the competitions. And that's just what they started doing. In jiu-jitsu competitions, my guys began chucking their opponents right and left, landing in the impact control position, and then instantly transitioning to a submission. One of my fifteen-year-old blue belts started landing flying attacks. I took twenty of my guys to the US Open, and ten of them won gold medals. Most of the others took either second or third place. After the competition, Joao Pierini, a jiu-jitsu black belt, came up to me and asked about my secret to success. I told him that I had excellent students and kept an open mind when it came to training. I had created an environment that was anything but a dictatorship, and my students excelled as a result.

JUDO VERSUS JIU-JITSU

In my opinion, you can only go so far in judo when learning from an instructor who thinks jiu-jitsu has nothing to offer, and you can only go so far with jiu-jitsu when learning from an instructor who thinks judo has nothing to offer. It is impossible to decide which art is better because they both have their strengths. It doesn't take a martial arts mastermind to discover what those strengths are—all it takes is a close look at the rules that govern each of the radically different sports.

In judo you score high points by throwing your opponent through the air. And if you can toss your opponent squarely on his back, the crowd will cheer, the ref will raise your hand, and you'll walk off the mat the victor. As a result, you can step into any judo academy in the country and ninety percent of the time you'll see the students honing their grip fighting and throws. The other ten percent of the time you'll see them focusing on their groundwork, but it's not the type of grappling that you will find in a jiu-jitsu academy. In judo there is a limited amount of time to finish an opponent on the mat before the referee restarts the fight in the standing position. If they used small, calculated movements like jiu-jitsu practitioners to achieve a dominant position, they would have no time left over to go for a finish. Instead they use the strength and speed they developed over hundreds of hours of grip fighting and throwing to hunt aggressively for a submission. The

byproduct is that judo players generally have limited technique on the ground. I'm sure there are plenty of judoka who would disagree with this, but they have no basis from which to argue. They don't understand the true meaning of ground technique because they don't do anything slowly. Every time they step onto the mat, it becomes a war of attributes.

Although jiu-jitsu stemmed from judo, the sport has taken a completely different path because of the rules of jiu-jitsu competition. Even though jiu-jitsu matches start in the standing position, there isn't this big emphasis on throws because once the fight hits the mat, it tends to stay there for a prolonged period of time. The referee doesn't stand the fight up if the action slows, which makes technical groundwork more important than technical throws. Walk into any jiu-jitsu academy, and ninety percent of the time you'll find the students rolling on the mat, working on gaining ground one inch at a time. With their primary goal being trying to outwit their opponent rather than overpower him, they are on a constant quest to develop more efficient ways to transition to dominant positions and sink in submission holds.

When you look at the two disciplines in this rudimentary light, it becomes clear that each discipline has evolved in accordance with a specific set of rules. Judo is more technical on grip fighting and throws, and its players develop strength and speed. Jiu-jitsu is far more technical on the ground. If you combine the two, you plug the holes in each. Having the ability to chuck and out-grip your opponent certainly won't hurt you in jiu-jitsu competition, nor will being able to pull out technical submissions during a judo match. At the very least, it gives you options.

When I break it down like this for people, they understand how cross training will give them an advantage over almost every opponent who refuses to stray from the parameters of his discipline. The true challenge comes not with convincing judo players and jiu-jitsu practitioners that they have something to gain by incorporating the strengths of judo and jiu-jitsu to make their game more well-rounded, but rather convincing them to attack the new discipline in such a way that will allow them to reach their full potential.

REACHING YOUR FULL POTENTIAL

If you are a jiu-jitsu practitioner and want to improve your game by adding judo techniques to your repertoire, then you'll have to put your jiu-jitsu training aside and check your ego at the door while attending judo practice. It is the only way that you will reach your full potential. If you ignore my suggestion and embark into judo with your jiu-jitsu eyeglasses on, the sport will seem ridiculous. You'll ask yourself why you are trying to pin your opponent when there are no pins in jiu-jitsu. You'll wonder why you're learning throws such as seoi-nage, which gives your opponent an opportunity to take your back. Having biased opinions will only hold you back. You will make the most gains by learning judo as it applies to judo competition.

The same thing goes for judo players who wish to incorporate jiu-jitsu to better their game. Once I had my own program, I convinced several members of the San Jose State Judo Team that jiu-jitsu had something to offer them. They started coming to jiu-jitsu practice at AKA, and a few of them have made phenomenal gains. They did this by leaving their judo training at the door. Instead of applying their strength and aggression in jiu-jitsu practice, which would limit their potential to learn, they attack jiu-jitsu as a separate discipline. As a result, they walk away with technical knowledge that they can apply to their judo at a later date.

Training my students to attack the two disciplines separately has allowed them to become proficient in both. When it came time for me to show them how to combine the arts, it made perfect sense. It took them less than a day to learn how to do seoi-nage so an opponent couldn't take their back. It took them less than a day to combine their newfound attributes with their already existing technique and finesse. By the time they started entering competitions, they not only had a good understanding of both arts, but they also understood the most effective ways to integrate them. Guys who I cross-trained for just a couple of months started out-gripping all of their opponents at the competitions. They chucked competitors through the air, landed in the impact control position, and then immediately transitioned to a submission. They stopped wrestling shots because they had learned how to grip properly. And most importantly, they constantly took their opponents out of their comfort zone. If an opponent had strong ground skills, they used their judo to keep the fight standing and wear him out. If an opponent had strong stand-up skills, they took the fight to the mat and dominated with their jiu-jitsu. They didn't have to play into their opponent's hands because they had options. I organized this book in the same way I teach my students, and as long as you put on the correct eyeglasses for the tutorial, you should experience significant success.

THE NO GI CONTROVERSY

There has been an ongoing debate as to whether or not jiu-jitsu practitioners who wish to one day compete in MMA or no gi grappling tournaments should train with a gi. To me there is only one answer—Yes.

When I first came to AKA, I had trained with a gi most of my life. I wore a gi when I trained judo, and I wore a gi when training under Ralph Gracie. Sure there were times when I took the gi off, but the majority of the time I wore a jacket and pants and a belt every time I climbed onto the mats. At AKA I suddenly found myself among a bunch of world-class MMA competitors such as Josh Thomson, Josh Koscheck, Mike Swick, John Fitch, and Mike Van Arsdale. These guys were preparing for fights in the Ultimate Fighting Championship, and as their instructor, I had to cater to their needs, which was no gi grappling. After a year at AKA, I climbed onto the mats with Mike Kyle, who outweighed me by eighty pounds. In ten minutes, I tapped him five times. When I trained with Koscheck for the first time, I submitted him over and over again, and he was an NCAA wrestler. Although I had seldom trained without a gi, the transition was easy.

The reason it was so easy was because learning with the gi had taught me proper technique. When you learn without a gi, you slip and slide everywhere because of the sweat factor, and that makes you sloppy. Because you can't get solid grips, it forces you to focus more on attributes than technique, which makes it hard to learn how to use tiny movements to control your opponent's body. Once you have acquired those movements

by training with a gi, it doesn't take long to adapt your game to no gi grappling. Dozens of top-level MMA fighters have proven this, but many people will never get it. For example, I was reading the posts on MMA.tv recently, and a guy claimed that training with a gi created 'pussies'. I wanted to ask him if he thought BJ Penn was a pussy, because he trained most of his life in a gi. Did he think Karo Parisyan was a pussy, because he also grew up in a gi. I guess it all comes down to a simple question: 'Do you want to possess strength or do you want to possess technique?' I would much rather possess technique because strength is easily acquired. If you practice the judo techniques laid out in this book, then you will develop speed and strength. You could also do Cross Fit or another exercise routine to further boost your power. Technique is much harder to come by.

Eddie Bravo has been very outspoken about why people should train without a gi if they plan on entering MMA competition or no gi grappling tournaments. In his book *Jiu-Jitsu Unleashed*, he used the example of a wrestler versus a traditional jiu-jitsu practitioner. If you dressed them both in a gi, the wrestler would probably be in serious trouble, but if they went at it bareback, then the jiu-jitsu guy would probably be in serious trouble. I have no argument with that, but the guys at my academy don't train like traditional jiu-jitsu practitioners. Most jiu-jitsu practitioners train to win jiu-jitsu tournaments, and that is the most boring thing you can do with jiu-jitsu. Being a world champion, in my opinion, does not necessarily mean that you are good. You can stall in every single match and still become a world champion.

The jiu-jitsu guys Eddie is talking about are the ones who use the gi to excel in the context of winning jiu-jitsu tournaments. I don't teach my students to win tournaments. Do we win? Yes. But we win on taps. If someone trains to win tournaments, they are not going to reach their full potential because a large part of winning tournaments depends upon your ability to stall when you're ahead on points. Winning tournaments is a great way to build a career and a name, but the problem arises when tournament winners decide to use their name to enter MMA competition. They step into the ring or cage with the same strategy they used to win jiu-jitsu tournaments. Lacking the proper training method needed to flourish, they sometimes do poorly.

It is important to recognize that when well-known jiu-jitsu practitioners enter the UFC and are unsuccessful, it has nothing to do with the fact that they train with a gi. What made them unsuccessful is that they had spent their time training to win jiu-jitsu competitions. If you train like my students, then you will not be passive. You will go for the

tap rather than the stall. And that comes from the best aspect of jiu-jitsu, which is the technique, and the best aspect of judo, which is pure aggression. When you mix the two philosophies, making the transition to no gi grappling is easy. You will be able to match the strength of opponents who have trained without a gi since day one, and outmatch them with your technique. If you doubt what I'm saying, just look at guys like BJ Penn and Karo Parisyan. They both learned with a gi, and they're reaping havoc in the UFC. Even Eddie Bravo's instructor Jean Jacques Machado, an Abu Dhabi Champion and one of the best no-gi grapplers out there, learned technique by wearing a uniform.

SECTION ONE

INCORPORATING JUDO AND JIU-JITSU

ROLLS

Every practitioner of the grappling arts is bound to get thrown or swept at one time or another. Although it is important to understand how to counter throws and sweeps, it is just as important to know how to react when you're caught off guard.

When your body is cast unwillingly upside down, it is easy to lose track of your limbs and even your opponent, which can be a recipe for disaster. I see it happen all the time. A guy gets swept, and because he has no idea of how to roll with the sweep, he flails his arms away from his body in an attempt to regain his balance, giving his opponent an easy armlock. I have also seen guys get thrown on their face. If they had just taken the time to learn how to roll, they would have saved themselves humiliation and pain.

Conducting rolling drills will help you keep your limbs close to your body and maintain your bearings when getting thrown or swept, which limits potential injury and makes it much harder for your opponent to catch you in a submission. Rolls are also the first step in learning how to land properly, which will be very beneficial when you start incorporating throws into your game. Practicing rolls will even help you escape submissions. I've seen countless competitors over the years tap to armlocks they could have avoided with a roll. And if you should one day find yourself flying over the handlebars of a motorcycle, just as my brother did, having rolls ingrained in your frontal lobe might save your life. If my brother hadn't pulled out a flawless judo roll as his head neared the pavement, he probably would have done the photos for this book in a diaper rather than a gi. Although fifteen minutes of rolling drills at the start of practice might seem tedious, the benefits are well worth the minimal investment of time and energy.

FORWARD ROLL

It is important to note that acquiring this basic forward roll is the first step in learning how to properly break a fall, which you will be getting into soon enough. When executing this drill you want keep your limbs tight to your body to avoid injury. If one of your arms gets left behind, you could tear a rotator cuff or hand your opponent a submission. It is also extremely important to keep your chin tucked to your chest to avoid hurting your neck. Focusing on all of this at once might be difficult in the beginning, but if you spend five minutes with this drill at the start of every practice, rolling back and forth across the mat, the movement will quickly become instinctual. Once you've got down the basics, make sure that you are rolling in a straight line. If you are constantly veering into your classmates, then you likely have too much weight on one foot or your head is to one side rather than centered between your knees.

1 I begin my forward roll movement by standing on one edge of the mat. My feet are spread a shoulder's width apart, my hands are by my sides, and I'm looking in the direction I'm going to roll.

2 Dropping down into a squat position, I shift my weight slightly forward and place my fingertips on the mat.

3 As I push myself forward with my feet, I bend my elbows and tuck my chin to my chest. You don't want to keep your head up because it will plant on the mat and your body will keep going. Instead of angling my elbows to the outside, I have pressed them tightly against my knees to turn my body into a ball that will roll with ease.

4 I am in the middle of my roll. Notice how my body has become almost round. I keep my elbows to my knees and my chin tucked. This allows the momentum of my initial push off to send me across my back and back up toward my feet. Dropping my head or letting an arm flail out would decrease the momentum of the roll and make me vulnerable to injury or a submission.

5 Having kept my momentum, I roll up onto my feet. My head is slightly in front of my knees to maintain balance, and my elbows are still tucked to my knees. From here, I can either stand up or enter into another roll.

6 I finish by standing. Since I have done the movement properly, my hands are by my sides, my feet are slightly spread, and I am looking forward.

BACKWARD ROLL

When you're walking down the street and trip, you have several options other than executing a forward roll. You can bend your knees to lessen the impact or stretch out into a lunge to catch yourself. When falling backwards, your only good option is to break your fall, and developing a backward roll is the first part of learning how to do that properly. If you practice this drill on a regular basis, then you will be better prepared for when you get caught in a backward throw like osoto-gari. You will also be more efficient at pulling guard on an advancing opponent, executing sweeps, and landing throws such as tomoe-nage, which requires rolling to your back. And having a good backward roll will limit your potential for neck injury while doing all of the above. Spending five minutes with backward rolls at the beginning of practice might seem like overkill, but when you get into throws you'll quickly recognize the payoff.

1 Starting in the squat position, I keep my elbows tucked to my knees to turn my body into a ball. I also have my head slightly in front of my knees, which will help generate momentum when I move backwards into the roll.

2 Rolling backwards, I grab my knees and keep my elbows tucked against my body. This will not only keep my body balled up, but also prevent injury and lessen my chance of getting caught in a submission.

3 Turning my head to my right side to avoid injuring my neck, I roll the weight of my body between my head and shoulder. My hands come down to the mat because I will need them to help guide my body back up to the squat position. In the beginning, it might be hard to roll in a straight line because of how you're turning your head, but after a few weeks you'll slowly learn how to compensate.

4 Having used my hands to push off, I come back up to the squat position. Notice how my elbows are still pressed tightly to my knees. From here I'm ready to execute another backward roll.

FORWARD ROLL WITH SPREAD LEGS

Now that you have acquired a basic forward and backward roll, it is time to step things up a notch and learn how to use your body to generate momentum in a roll. It is nice when you turn into your opponent for a throw and catch him off guard, making your throw effortless, but most of the time your opponent will put up some kind of resistance. In such cases you'll often have to over-exaggerate your throw to be successful, which means casting your body into a forward or backward roll. This will be very hard to achieve if you don't understand how to generate momentum with your body. Practicing the forward roll with spread legs will help you acquire this skill. It will also help prepare you for getting thrown fast and hard by an opponent. If you've never headed into a forward or backward roll with speed, and then in competition you find yourself heading into one at fifty miles per hour, you could lose your bearings and get caught in a submission. The more you practice this drill, the more comfortable you'll become at generating and dealing with speed while rolling.

1 I begin my forward roll movement by standing on one edge of the mat. My feet are spread a shoulder's width apart, my hands are by my sides, and I'm looking in the direction I'm going to roll.

2 My movement here is the same as a basic forward roll. I squat down, move my head slightly in front of my knees, and plant my hands on the mat so I can set the speed of the roll.

3 To start the roll, I lower my upper body down to the mat by bending my elbows. My chin is tucked toward my chest and my elbows are on the inside of my knees to turn my body into a ball. On this one, I am going to push off with my feet a little harder to generate the momentum needed to end the roll with my legs spread.

4 As I move into my roll, I have more momentum than I did with the basic forward roll. Keeping my elbows tucked into my body, I gradually separate my legs as they near the mat.

5 Having spread my legs out to the sides, I drop my hands to the mat and push off, gaining extra momentum to prop myself up.

6 I finish with my legs spread in the standing position. From here, I am going to keep my legs spread and squat down for another roll. However, the moment I push off with my feet, I am going to bring my legs back together for the roll. They won't separate again until they are about to touch down on the other side of the roll. This will help build coordination.

BACKWARD ROLL WITH SPREAD LEGS

A lot of times when an opponent chucks you with a backwards throw, he will either lose his grips on your gi or try to establish different grips as the two of you land. You'll have a small window of opportunity to escape to a dominant position or back to your feet, but it can be difficult to capitalize on that opportunity if you don't understand how to generate momentum with your body during the roll. This drill will help you acquire that skill.

1 Starting with my heels against the edge of the mat, I keep my hands by my sides and my feet spread a shoulder's width apart.

2 I squat down with my weight slightly over my knees to maintain balance. Unlike with the forward roll, my hands aren't going to touch the mat.

3 Pushing off with my feet, I roll backwards. To turn my body into a ball, I keep my chin and knees tucked toward my chest and my elbows tucked close to my body.

4 Spreading my legs at the last moment, I place my hands on the mat with my elbows bent to help push myself up. Notice that my elbows are still tucked toward my body.

FORWARD ROLL WITH HANDSTAND

Continuing to climb up the rolling ladder, we move onto the forward roll with handstand. Along with increasing your coordination and ability to control momentum, this drill will also teach you how to take the impact out of a throw. If you can successfully conduct a forward roll from a handstand, then you can successfully manage a roll when being thrown three feet into the air. The next step is jumping into a roll. Once you make that transition, you'll be able to get thrown thirty times a night and still wake up the following morning and go to work. But it is important to not try and progress too quickly. With potential injury on the line, you must not reach for the next rung until you have a firm grasp on the last.

1 I begin my forward roll movement by standing on one edge of the mat. My feet are spread a shoulder's width apart, my hands are by my side, and I'm looking in the direction I'm going to roll.

2 My movement here is the same as a basic forward roll. I squat down, move my head slightly in front of my knees, and plant my hands on the mat so I can kick by body up into a handstand. Notice how my elbows are slightly bent—this will not change when I go up into the handstand.

3 Pushing off with my feet, I move into a handstand. It is important that your feet don't go too fast or slow over the top. You want just enough speed so you hesitate for a split second at the top, and then move into the roll. My elbows have stayed slightly bent. Instead of dropping from this height, I will slowly bend my elbows to lower my head toward the mat as I head into the roll. It is important that you keep tension in your arms as you do this. You don't want to relax your arms all at once because then your head will pile-drive into the mat. My students do this from time to time, and it is a good way to end up with a neck injury.

4 As my elbows bend to lower my head to the mat, I tuck my chin to my chest and bring my knees toward my head. This turns my body into a ball and allows me to roll gently across the mat.

5 Because my knees are moving with such momentum, I grasp them with my hands. This not only eliminates some of the speed of my lower body, but also increases the speed of my upper body and helps propel me up to my feet.

6 Using the momentum of the roll, I come up to a squat position. After an ample amount of practice, you should be able to attain this position without falling forward or backward. From here, you can choose to continue forward into another roll or stand up and finish the drill.

BACKWARD ROLL WITH HANDSTAND

The basic backwards roll got you comfortable rolling in a direction that you can't see, which is extremely important because it allows you to maintain your equilibrium and control in a normally awkward situation. Practicing the backward roll with handstand will continue to increase your coordination, as well as further prepare you for being thrown full force during a match.

1 Starting with my heels against the edge of the mat, I keep my hands by my sides and my feet spread a shoulder's width apart.

2 I squat down with my weight slightly over my knees to maintain balance. Unlike the forward roll, my hands don't touch the mat.

3 I push off my feet with enough force to execute the roll and pop up into a handstand. Here my hands are preparing to leave my knees so that I can place them on the mat by my head and force my body upright. It is very important to remain balled up during the roll. If your body is straight, the handstand won't be possible. To avoid injuring your neck, it is also important to turn your head to one side so that you roll between your head and shoulder.

4 Using the momentum of my body and the strength in my arms, I pop up into a handstand and straighten my body as much as possible.

5 Letting my legs kick over the top of my head, I land in somewhat of a squat position with my knuckles on the ground.

6 I finish the movement by standing up, and then I instantly move into another backwards roll with handstand.

FALLS

If you start executing throws without first learning how to properly fall, then you should expect to endure injury and pain. When getting thrown, the idea is to minimize the damage to the critical areas of your body such as your head and back by absorbing the majority of the impact with your non-critical areas such as your arms and legs. Practicing the following drills will help teach you how to do that. Once you feel comfortable falling, you should be ready to move onto throws, but it is important that you do so cautiously.

Because I have been training judo since the age of five, I can climb onto the mat with someone who has never done any martial arts and slam him to the ground without causing him any pain. I can do this because I understand the mechanics of a throw; I can direct my opponent's body to the mat in such a way that will lessen the impact.

Obviously during a real fight my goal will be the opposite. Instead of being gentle with my opponent, my goal will be to inflict damage. I could abandon the throw in mid-air and drop my opponent onto his head. If the fight occurs out in the street, I could toss my aggressor into a fire hydrant or throw him hard onto the pavement, breaking his back. There are plenty of options to cause damage to your opponent with a throw, but that should be learned later. In the beginning, you want to learn proper falling techniques without taking major impacts or suffering injuries, which means training with a veteran or taking things very, very slowly. If you are learning on a mat at home with a brother or friend, then both of you should pay special attention to throwing each other as gently as possible in the beginning. All it takes is one bad fall to mess up a perfectly good day.

RIGHT AND WRONG SHOULDER ROLL

Now that you have a thorough understanding of how to roll forwards and backwards a variety of different ways, you should be ready to learn how to execute a shoulder roll, which is the most commonly used technique for breaking a fall on a forward throw. If done right, it will take the energy generated by your opponent's throw and disperse it throughout the non-critical points of your body. Earlier I talked about my brother doing a forward roll when he crashed on his motorbike. I did the same with a shoulder roll. The first time on a motorcycle, I hit a bump and went flying like superman over my handlebars. Without thinking, I executed a shoulder roll. I stood up a second later and dusted myself off. There were no persisting neck or back problems. No face rash. No broken bones.

In addition to possibly one day saving your life, the shoulder roll will help you on an everyday basis in judo and jiu-jitsu. With as many times as I have been thrown, I would be in a wheelchair right now if not for this technique. I acquired the move in judo, but many jiu-jitsu practitioners also learn the shoulder roll in their first months of training. The problem is they usually learn it wrong. Because jiu-jitsu matches are generally a lot slower and gentler than Judo matches, jiu-jitsu practitioners finish the roll with their legs positioned close together because it gives them the leverage to pop up to their knees or feet after being thrown. However, if a jiu-jitsu practitioner attempted such a sloppy shoulder roll when thrown by a good judoka, he would probably pay a stiff price. It is imperative that your legs are extended and spread to maximize the amount of force taken out of the throw. The closer your legs are to one another, the less impact they absorb. In the beginning, I teach all my students to spread their limbs and stay down. After they have the basic movements ingrained and have learned the dynamics of taking the sting out of a hard throw, they can then begin tweaking their landing on a per-throw basis. If they get thrown hard, they land with their legs spread. If they get thrown softly, they can keep their legs closer together.

1 Starting at one edge of the mat, I keep my hands by my sides and my feet spread a shoulder's width apart.

2 Because I have decided to do a left shoulder roll, I take a step forward with my left foot. As I slowly bend my left knee to lower my body toward the mat, I extend my left arm out over my knee because my hand will be the first part of my body to touch the ground. It is important that you don't drop into the shoulder roll from a standing position—you want to gradually lower yourself with your front knee so that it is a smooth transition.

3 The first thing I do in this picture is set my left hand flat on the mat so that my fingers are pointed toward my right foot. If you notice, I have created an arch that starts in my fingers, goes up and around the crook in my arm, and then across my back. As I head into the roll, my body will roll across this arch and eliminate the majority of the force behind the throw. If I had placed my left hand down with my fingers pointing in the direction my body will travel, I would bend my fingers back as I headed into the roll. So once I have my left hand placed in the proper position, I then place my right hand on top of my left. Both of my elbows are going to bend as I lower my body into the roll. It is important not to relax your arms and drop directly down into the roll from this position because it increases the possibility of injuring your shoulder.

4 Pushing off with my right foot to create momentum, I follow the arch that I created with my left arm in the previous photo. Here I have just rolled off my arm and onto my left shoulder. My left knee has touched the ground, pushing my body slightly forward to get added momentum. My right knee is up in the air from having kicked my weight forward. It is important to notice that my head is tucked toward my right shoulder to allow my body to roll and avoid a neck injury.

5 Still continuing on the arch, the left side of my body leaves the mat as I move onto my right shoulder blade. To absorb the momentum of the throw, I'm preparing to strike the mat with my right leg, left foot, and right hand simultaneously. Notice that my right elbow is still bent and my right palm is facing the mat. Since my left hand will not be needed upon impact, I grab onto my right collar. This will not only keep it tight to my body upon impact, but also hinder my opponent from latching onto it and attempting an armlock. It is important to keep your chin tucked tightly to your chest. If you relax your neck, your head will most likely snap into the ground when you break the fall.

6 This is the proper way to break a fall. At the same time, my right hand, left foot, and right leg slap down on the mat. My right hand is palm down and several inches away from my right knee. My left foot lands flat on the canvas with my left knee pointed straight up. My right leg lands on its side. It is extremely important to notice that my right leg is spread away from my left leg. My left hand is still latched onto my gi, elbow tucked tight to my body, and I have kept tension in my neck to keep my head from whipping into the mat. When done properly, you should be able to get thrown on dirt or cement and walk away without injury.

7 This is the way many jiu-jitsu practitioners land. If you were taught to fall this way, it won't take much to correct your form. The only thing out of place in this photo is my right leg, which is tucked underneath my left leg. Although this positioning will help me rise back to my feet after a throw, it can have serious consequences. If I was thrown with enough force, my left leg might collapse upon impact and come crashing down on my right foot. In addition to this, I am limiting the amount of force my right leg takes away upon impact. I'm nearly cutting it in half. Landing the proper way on a good throw can be painful, but landing this way could mean a trip to the hospital. It is critical that your right leg is spread away from your left to absorb as much of your momentum as possible. After dealing with the throw, you can then worry about getting back up to your feet.

SIDE TO SIDE FALL

Practicing the side-to-side fall will help teach you how to take the impact out of a throw on both sides of your body. It will also improve your coordination and timing, allowing you to strike the mat with both legs and one arm at the same time. If you have an injured hand, you can use this drill to learn how to absorb the majority of the impact with your feet. If you have an injured foot, you can use the drill to learn how to absorb the impact with your opposite foot and hand. Side to side falls should be done slowly for at least a minute straight at the start of practice if you are just starting out. Intermediate practitioners can do it a little faster. If you've already been doing falls for quite some time, then you probably won't need to do this drill at all because intense shoulder rolls will already be a part of your everyday practice.

1 To begin the drill, I start in the landing position on my right side. My left foot is flat on the ground with my knee pointing up. My right leg is lying on its side and spread away from my left leg. My right hand is lying palm down on the mat, and my left hand is gripping the collar of my gi to take it out of the equation. Just as before, I keep my chin tucked to my chest.

2 Pushing off with my right foot, I roll my body to my left. Now that I am going to be landing on my left side, I grab the collar of my gi with my right hand and prepare to slap the mat with my left hand. I am also going to change my feet. This time, my right foot will land flat with my right knee pointing up.

3 Coming down onto my left side, I slap the mat with my left hand, right foot, and left leg at the same time. My left hand is palm down, and my left leg is absorbing the impact from my hip down to my heel. I have continued to grip my collar with my right hand and keep my head tightly tucked to my chest. From here, I am going to transition back to my right side.

BACK FALL

The back fall involves the same movement as a backward roll, but instead of rolling up onto your feet, you're going to slap your hands down on the mat to lessen the impact of the throw. This is an excellent way to break your fall when your opponent executes a kouchi-gari, ouchi-gari, or a sweep from the standing position. It is also a good way to break your fall from several open guard sweeps.

Although it might seem silly breaking a fall from such minimal height, the potential for injury is too great to try and learn this technique by jumping onto your back. If you practice this drill until you reach the intermediate level, you will slowly lose your fear of falling backwards, which will come in tremendously handy when you start incorporating flying attacks into your game.

1 Starting at one edge of the mat, I keep my hands at my sides and my feet spread a shoulder's width apart.

2 Dropping down into a squat position, I tighten my body because I know there is an impact coming. My elbows are on the outside of my knees because I will use them to break my fall.

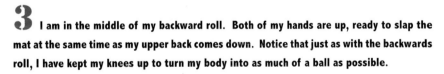

3 I am in the middle of my backward roll. Both of my hands are up, ready to slap the mat at the same time as my upper back comes down. Notice that just as with the backwards roll, I have kept my knees up to turn my body into as much of a ball as possible.

4 As my upper back comes down, I slap the mat with both hands at the same time. Just as with the shoulder roll, I want my arms spread out to maximize the amount of force I take out of the throw. The closer your arms are to your body, the more impact your back will take. It is also important to keep your chin tucked tightly to your chest to stop your head from whipping into the mat.

SIDE FALL

Although you'll land the same way as you did in the shoulder roll, I put this technique last because it takes a bit more coordination and you tend to land harder. It is the next step up the ladder to actually getting thrown. It still won't prepare you for getting thrown hard, but it will prepare you for getting thrown lightly. Everything is baby-steps when it comes to throwing, and practicing the side fall is one step that shouldn't be ignored.

The path your body makes when doing this drill is almost the exact path your body will make when you get foot swept by an opponent or execute a foot sweep on an opponent. As a result, the drill not only teaches you how to land safely when you get caught, but it also teaches you to spot a foot sweep coming, which is a big weakness of most jiu-jitsu practitioners. Over the years I have swept hundreds of jiu-jitsu practitioners who didn't know what I was doing until it was too late. It is a chink you don't want in your armor.

1 With my hands at my sides, I place my left foot slightly in front of my right. Because my first action will be on my left side, my eyes are directed toward my left foot. Anytime you do an action, your eyes want to be facing that direction.

2 I push off with my right foot to take a step forward with my left foot. Because my left hand will not be needed to break my fall, it's already latched onto the collar of my gi, keeping my arm coiled into my body.

3 Distributing my weight onto my left leg, I sweep my right foot forward across the mat. Notice that my big toe has lifted up and my pinky toe is scrapping the mat. This movement is identical to when you execute a foot sweep because it's the best way to snatch your opponent's leg. The only difference between this movement and an actual foot sweep is here you don't have a grip on your opponent's gi

4 I continue the sweeping motion and lift my right foot off the mat. If this had been an actual foot sweep, I would have brought my opponent's leg up with my right foot. It is important to notice that my left leg is bent. From here, I don't want to fall down to the mat. I want to lower myself down by continuing to bend my left leg. My right hand has come up in preparation to slap the mat, and my eyes are looking in the direction that my body is heading.

5 Lowering my body to the ground, I land in the break fall position. My left leg is still bent, and my right leg and right hand have just broken my fall. Notice that my chin is still tucked to my chest and my left hand is still gripping the collar of my gi.

GRIPS

Being a good grip fighter is huge in the grappling arts. Obtaining a dominant grip is the start to everything—throws, transitions, submissions, and flying attacks. Jiu-jitsu practitioners usually spend some time developing their grips, but not nearly to the extent of judo players. A good judoka will spend hours each week grip fighting with a partner, struggling to obtain the collar or high grip. Through such diligence, they develop speed, precision, and strength. The moment they get their grips, they take command. And when the fight goes to the ground, they bring their attributes with them. They can dominate their jiu-jitsu opponent with their gripping speed. They can overpower their jiu-jitsu opponent with their gripping strength. They can more easily execute a sweep or transition to a submission because their grips are so hard to break. Grips are the beginning to almost every single technique in the grappling arts, and there is no better discipline to develop your grips than judo. If you are strong in the gripping department, your overall game *will* improve.

SLEEVE GRIP

The Sleeve grip is the first technique in this section because it is generally the first grip that you'll be able to attain in a match. The reason for this is simple—when sparring with an opponent, generally the first part of his body you'll come into contact with are his hands. Hands can be very hard to grab, but sleeves aren't. You can certainly bypass your opponent's sleeve by stepping in and reaching for his collar, but in the process you'll usually expose a sleeve for him to grab. It works the other way around as well. If your opponent tries to reach past your hands for your collar, it is relatively easy to intercept his reaching arm by latching onto his sleeve.

Every judoka uses the following sleeve grip, no matter how experienced he is. At first it is important to acquire the basic hand movement, but soon you'll want to focus on the positioning of your sleeve grip. Every gi has a seam that runs down the sleeve. If you can crunch that seam between your fingers and palm as you make your grip, you will be on the strongest part of the sleeve and have the most control over your opponent's arm.

1 As my brother reaches in for my collar, I intercept his arm by cupping my hand around the seam running down the length of his sleeve.

2 I tighten my grip by coiling my fingers around the inside of my brother's sleeve, while at the same time driving in with my palm. If your opponent's sleeve has a bunch of slack around the forearm, you are most likely not driving in enough with your palm. When done right, your opponent's sleeve should resemble the sleeve of a tight sweater. The tighter the grip, the more control you will have over his arm. It is important to notice that I am not using my thumb. If I used my thumb, I would not be able to drive my palm forward because my thumb would get in the way. Here I have total control. If my brother doesn't move his arm, I can drive his arm down and out of the picture or pull it up to go for a throw. If he pulls his arm away, I am going to pull it back toward me. In the beginning, it is best to do the opposite of what your opponent does to keep his arm under control. I use this technique a lot in my Guerrilla Jiu-Jitsu ground game to gain the initiative for an attack.

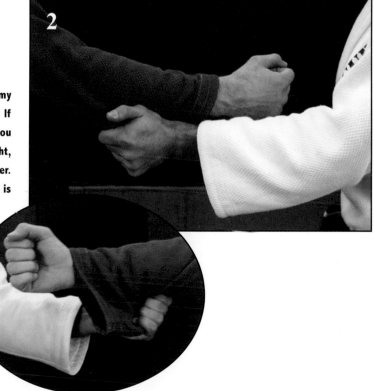

PISTOL GRIP

The pistol grip is the second grip judo players learn. It is generally used to latch onto an opponent's collar, and it works great in conjuncture with the sleeve grip because it allows you to reach your ultimate goal of controlling both sides of your opponent's body. So if you assume a sleeve grip on your opponent's left arm, then you will want to secure a pistol grip on his right collar. This gives you control of his circular motion, making it easier to throw him off balance and destroy his base. And with a good pistol grip there are plenty of throws at your disposal, including osoto-gari, harai-goshi, an assortment of foot sweeps, kouchi-gari, and ouchi-gari. If you spend some time grip fighting and developing a good pistol grip, becoming proficient at throws will be a lot easier. Eventually your movement will become so sharp that you can throw an opponent with a pistol grip alone, but in the beginning it is best to combine it with a sleeve grip because the duel holds will increase your offense and defense.

1 Reaching out, I dig the pinky, ring, and middle fingers of my right hand deep into the outside of my brother's collar. It is important to notice that my index finger and thumb are not a part of the group—they remain on the outside.

2 Grabbing a handful of my brother's collar with my first three fingers, I coil my fingers into my palm. At the same time, I drop my elbow. This is key because in many throws you will need your elbow connecting with your opponent's body. If I had grabbed with my index finger and thumb, my wrist would bend as I lowered my elbow, which would weaken my hold. You want your wrist solid and straight.

HIGH GRIP

Now that you have an understanding of the sleeve and pistol grip, it is time to get a little more advanced and work on developing a high grip. It is more advanced because it often requires moving one of your elbows away from your body, which in judo and jiu-jitsu creates a weakness that your opponent can capitalize on. For this reason, shorter judoka tend to favor controlling their opponent's chest with a pistol grip because it doesn't require them to reach. Taller judoka don't have to worry about this as much, and they often employ a high grip because it allows them to control their opponent's head. And any time you control your opponent's head, you also control his body. It doesn't mean that you should ignore the high grip if you happen to be short. I am considered quite short when compared to the other competitors in my weight division, yet I utilize the high grip almost as often as I utilize a pistol grip. Uchi-mata is one of my favorite throws, and it is generally executed off a high grip. I also have a host of foot sweeps I do with a high grip. The way shorter people can get away with this is by constantly working on developing their speed. If you can execute your throw faster than your opponent can capitalize on your weakness, you'll be successful. You might find that you like the pistol grip better, but having a high grip tucked into your arsenal will give you options.

1 My brother and I are in a somewhat of a neutral position. I have a sleeve grip on his right arm, and he has a collar grip. Most of the time in Judo the moment you grab your opponent, he too will grab something to level out the playing field. It can be frustrating, but that's just how the game is played. To get the upper hand, I have decided to go for a high grip on my brother's collar. This can be tricky because as I go for the grip my brother will try to grab my sleeve. Whoever wins this little battle will have a good chance of getting a throw.

2 In order to break through my brother's defenses and obtain a high grip, I tuck my left elbow into my body and then simultaneously snap my hips in a counterclockwise direction and tug on his sleeve with my left hand. This not only sets me up for a throw, but it also turns my brother's body in a counterclockwise direction and drops his defenses for a split second. In that small window of opportunity, I shoot my right hand explosively forward almost like I'm throwing a right cross. Instead of throwing my fist into his face, however, I dig my thumb underneath his collar. People have different preferences as to where to place the thumb behind the collar. Some like to dig it in more toward the shoulder, and others directly behind the neck. I tend to like somewhere between the neck and shoulder.

3 After tightening a wad of my brother's gi between my palm and fingers, I pull my right hand toward me to disrupt my brother's base. At the same time, I drop my right elbow down into his body. In this particular photo, I have an extreme right stance, which means that my body is turned toward my brother's right shoulder. Here my body is already halfway in, which sets me up for a right forward throw. My entire body is tight. If my elbow was up on my right side, then I would be vulnerable on that side and my grip would mean next to nothing. My brother could attempt a foot sweep from here, but I am keeping sharp and anticipating his movements. Judo is similar to kickboxing in that anytime two fighters get close to one another, they are both vulnerable to attack. It just so happens that here I have the upper hand. I am in command because I have gotten my grips first. My brother could obtain a grip with his left hand and level the playing field, but by then I should have already completed my throw.

4 This is a reverse shot showing the high grip and dropped elbow. Dropping the elbow is extremely important because it stops my brother from stepping into me with a throw of his own. If I were to lift my elbow up, he could close the distance in a split second and I'd have to abandon my throw and play more defensively. In this case, it's my agenda that is being pushed.

BREAKING COLLAR GRIP

Occasionally your opponent will be able to sneak one of his hands past your guard and latch onto your collar. If you have already obtained grips of your own and feel confident that you can beat your opponent to a throw, sometimes his grip won't bother you. Your ultimate goal is to push your agenda without allowing your opponent to push his. You always want to be in control, and if your opponent is stealing that control by latching onto your collar, the chances are you will want to break his grip and turn the tide of battle in the process. This is an excellent technique to do just that.

1 My brother has managed to sneak his right hand past my guard and latch onto my collar with a pistol grip. You may think it odd that he is using his index finger to grab, but that is because he is farther away, and it is nearly impossible for him to throw me from this distance. If he managed to get closer, he would assume a pistol grip by pulling his index finger out of my collar, which would allow him to drop his elbow. But I will not let him do that. Here he is one move ahead of me, so I am going to break his grip.

2 I reach my left hand forward and secure a sleeve grip just above my brother's elbow. My goal behind this is to secure his arm in place so I can effectively break his grip. Notice how my brother's gi is nice and tight around his biceps. The tighter my grip on his sleeve, the more control I'll have of his arm. If my brother tries to step in, I can extend my left arm to keep him at bay.

3 Controlling the distance between my brother's body and mine with my left hand, I latch onto the inside of his sleeve with my right hand. If my brother is determined to push past the blockade I created with my left arm, I will step back and circle around to maintain distance.

4 Determined to break my brother's collar grip, I slide my left hand down from his elbow and grip on the outside of his sleeve. Both of my palms are pressing into his wrist, and both of my elbows are pressed tight against my body to maintain strong posture.

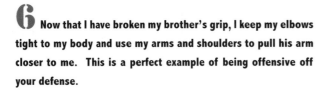

5 Still with my elbows locked to my body, I drive my palms down and away. At the same time, I push off with my front leg to drive my weight back. The combined effort is enough to break my brother's grip on my collar. To keep him from re-grabbing, I lock my arms straight.

6 Now that I have broken my brother's grip, I keep my elbows tight to my body and use my arms and shoulders to pull his arm closer to me. This is a perfect example of being offensive off your defense.

7 Because I have gained control of my brother's right arm, I have free access to his back. Letting go of his sleeve with my left hand, I take a step forward and reach around for a high grip. On my brother's left shoulder, I establish my grip on the seam that connects his left sleeve to the main part of his gi. Now that I have both a high grip and a sleeve grip, my brother has something to contend with. From here I can execute a sweep or a number of different throws. I have taken control of the fight.

BREAKING HIGH GRIP

When you go up against a judoka and he obtains a high grip, the chances are he is proficient with it. This is especially true when your opponent is taller than you. My brother has several inches on me, and when he latches on with a high grip, my first instinct is to break it. If I let him keep it, he will have control of my head and movement, which is not an option. There are several ways to break a high grip, but I have found the following technique to be the most efficient. Of course it is even better to intercept your opponent's hand before he can get his hold, but unfortunately that isn't always an option when engaged in a high-speed grip-fighting battle.

1 My brother and I are approaching each other, searching for grips.

2 My brother lashes out for a high grip. My best option would be to put up my left hand to block his high grip. I could do that by either latching onto his sleeve with my left hand or simply knocking his arm off its path. But because my brother is tall, it's a straight shot for him to obtain a high grip. Here he is too fast and penetrates my defense before I can intercept his arm. It is important that I don't hesitate—the moment his hand lands, I want to react.

3 I reach up to control my brother's sleeve with both hands just as I did when breaking a normal collar grip. Both of my elbows are locked tight to my body. If he moves forward, I want to move back to keep distance between us and to stop him from securing a second grip. If he moves back, I want to hold my ground because I could be stepping right into a throw.

4 I lock my grip down on either side of my brother's right sleeve, applying pressure into his wrist with my palms. At the same time, I turn my head in a clockwise direction. Although this movement is slight, it limits my brother's control over my head, which increases my chances of breaking his grip. However, it is important not to dip too far down because then your opponent can push your head toward the mat and possibly move around and take your back.

5 To break the hold completely, I use my shoulders and arms to force my brother's arm down and away. If he pulls his arm back toward his body, I will let go and start over from a neutral position. If I can maintain control of his arm, I will release my left grip and reach around his back for a high grip, just as I did in the previous move.

BREAKING COLLAR GRIP WITH HAND

Oftentimes you'll get into a situation where both you and your opponent have secured a collar grip. To get the advantage, you will need to secure a second grip or eliminate your opponent's collar grip. The most obvious way to achieve the latter is to snatch your opponent's sleeve with your free hand and force his arm away, but in the process you will expose your sleeve for you opponent to grab with his free hand. A safer method is to grab your own gi and rip your collar out of your opponent's grasp. With your free arm closer to your body, it will be much harder for your opponent to grab your sleeve.

1 Both my brother and I have obtained a collar grip. Because this is pretty much a neutral position, both of us are trying to get an inside grip. I could establish an inside grip by dropping my left elbow to the inside of my brother's right arm. My brother could get the inside grip by bringing his right elbow in, blocking me from dropping my left elbow. If he managed to do that, I would be vulnerable because he could then use the dominant positioning of his arm to lift my left elbow up and away from my body and step in for a throw. I don't feel comfortable engaging in this battle, so I decide to break his grip.

2 Notice that my brother is extreme right, meaning his right shoulder is forward, and I am extreme left, meaning my left shoulder is forward. I want to keep it that way. Bringing my right shoulder forward would give my bother an opportunity to secure a grip on the right side of my gi, as would bringing my right hand forward to break his grip. Maintaining distance between us by locking my left arm straight, I reach up with my right hand and grab ahold of my collar just below his hand. It is important that you don't simply grab your collar—you want to bend your wrist and gather the fabric up in your hand. This will give you leverage to rip your collar out of your opponent's grasp.

3 Continuing to stiff-arm my brother with my left arm to keep distance, I turn my right shoulder in a clockwise direction and use both my arm and shoulder to rip my collar from his grasp.

4 Keeping my right arm tucked against my torso and turning in a clockwise direction, I use my entire body to break my brother's grip on my collar. By keeping everything tight, my collar has become a part of my body, making it impossible for my brother to maintain his hold. It is important to notice that I have continued to straight-arm my brother to maintain distance. It is also important to notice that the fingers of my left hand have not bent back over my wrist because that would make my grip on my brother's collar weak. Instead, I am leading with my wrist. From here, I can turn into my brother and go right into a fireman's carry. If he decides to chaise me to reestablish his grip, I can drop down into a seoi-nage.

GETTING INSIDE GRIP

Getting the inside grip is key to controlling your opponent. If both you and your opponent have established a collar grip, as long as you obtain the inside grip, you'll have a distinct advantage. You can use your inside grip to hinder your opponent from executing a throw. You can use it to force your opponent's elbow up and then step in for a throw. The options are limitless. However, it is important to make a move quickly once you have the inside position because your window of opportunity will most likely be small. If you obtain the inside grip and are slow in attempting a move, your opponent will take it away from you. And if your opponent obtains the inside grip and you are slow taking it away from him, there is a good chance that you'll get thrown.

1 My brother and I have both obtained a collar grip. Although my arm is currently on the inside, my brother is in the process of dropping his elbow to the inside of my arm, which would give him the inside grip. He could then lift my left elbow up with his arm, making me vulnerable to a host of attacks.

2 Not wanting my brother to obtain a superior grip, I let go of his collar and circle my left arm around the outside of his right arm.

3 Once I have reestablished my grip on my brother's collar, we are back to neutral. We have essentially switched places, but now I have the ability to drop my elbow and secure the inside grip.

4 I drop my elbow to the inside of my brother's arm to secure the inside grip, taking away his power and leverage—basically nullifying his grip. I have latched onto his collar using all my fingers and thumb, but as I move closer I will transition to a pistol grip so I can drop my elbow into his body, making him even more vulnerable.

5 I display my control by lifting my brother's right elbow up using my left arm. Once his elbow is up and away from his body, he is extremely vulnerable. I can turn into a seoi-nage or jump to osoto-gari. However, it is important to note that my window of opportunity here is very small. My brother knows that his defenses are down, and he will immediately try to fight back to a neutral or dominant position. So here I am crouching down, preparing to make my move without hesitation.

6 I reach my right arm forward and obtain a standard sleeve grip on my brother's left arm. Now I have both sides of his body controlled. From here, I will change my left grip to a pistol grip and move right into a foot sweep or throw.

KEEPING INSIDE GRIP

Getting the inside grip is only half the battle. You must also learn how to keep it, which can be quite tricky. It is kind of like pummeling for the under-hooks in wrestling. Most of the time you will get the inside grip, your opponent will do some maneuvering to steal it away from you, and then you have to get it back. It goes back and forth like this until one of you can manage a throw. This is an excellent drill to practice because the hunt for the inside grip can occur at a million miles an hour. The more you practice this drill, the more dominant you will be when pummeling during practice and in competition.

1 My brother and I both have a collar grip, but because my left arm is blocking his right elbow from dropping down, I have the inside grip.

2 To capitalize on my dominant position, I force my brother's right elbow up with my left arm. By doing this, I am making him vulnerable on his right side and creating an opening to attack.

3 Before I can make my move, my brother lets go of my collar and circles his arm around the outside of my arm in hopes of reestablishing a collar grip with better positioning.

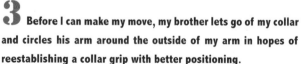

4 My brother gets his grip, and because his right arm is now blocking my left elbow from dropping, he has the inside grip.

5 Using his dominant grip against me, my brother forces my left elbow toward the ceiling with his right arm, making me weak on my left side.

6 Before my brother can attack, I let go of his collar and circle my arm around his arm.

7 Getting the inside grip again, I decide that I've had enough of this back and forth battle. Being more aggressive, I am about to lock down my inside grip on his left side. I begin by reaching my right hand toward his right collar.

8 To close the distance, I drop my left elbow toward my brother's body and take a step forward. At the same time, I secure an additional collar grip with my right hand. By keeping my left arm extremely bent and my right arm slightly bent, I create a shield with my arms, making it very difficult for my brother to circle his arm around and reestablish a more dominant grip. This puts me in an attack position.

BAIT GRIP

Now that you understand the basic grips and how to combine them, we're going to work on baiting an opponent by putting out a sleeve for him to grab. I do this often at the opening of a match to test my opponent's reactions and see if he will bite my hook. Usually my opponent realizes that I'm fishing, but oftentimes he'll still take the bait because he thinks he can outmatch my speed and power. And sometimes that is just what happens—this move will not work all of the time. But I like the technique because it captures my opponent's focus. It will tempt him, and if he decides to go for it, I am quick to react because I anticipated his movement. The anticipation part is key. You should never dangle a sleeve out and then get caught by surprise when your opponent grabs it. If you hold out the carrot, you have to be ready to draw it back and counterattack. It is an excellent technique for getting a match started in a hurry.

1 My brother and I are squared off, searching for an opening. I have already decided that I'm going to test his reactions by baiting him with a sleeve, so I'm preparing to close the distance.

2 I take a step forward with my left foot, holding my left arm up and out so my brother can easily latch onto the sleeve. This instantly snares his attention. Although I'm leaning forward, my left leg is bent, ready to push my body away. If my brother makes a move I don't like, such as ignoring my bait and reaching for a high grip, I won't hesitate to launch myself back. I will also use my raised hand to bat his reaching arm away.

3 My brother feels his speed and power is greater than mine and he takes the bait. Because of the angle of my arm, he reaches forward to get an underhand grip on my sleeve.

4 As my brother's fingers close around my sleeve, I rotate my hips in a counterclockwise direction and pull my left arm slightly back to ensure that he doesn't secure a really tight grip. (If you pull your arm too far back, your opponent will lose his grip and withdraw his arm). At the same time, I reach my right hand forward and grip his sleeve.

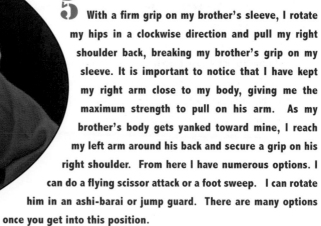

5 With a firm grip on my brother's sleeve, I rotate my hips in a clockwise direction and pull my right shoulder back, breaking my brother's grip on my sleeve. It is important to notice that I have kept my right arm close to my body, giving me the maximum strength to pull on his arm. As my brother's body gets yanked toward mine, I reach my left arm around his back and secure a grip on his right shoulder. From here I have numerous options. I can do a flying scissor attack or a foot sweep. I can rotate him in an ashi-barai or jump guard. There are many options once you get into this position.

BREAKING SLEEVE GRIP WITH KNEE

This is an excellent technique for breaking an opponent's grip on your sleeve in jiu-jitsu competition. The reason it doesn't work well in judo competition is because it is an illegal technique—and I have no idea why. It is a shame because not only is this a very quick move, but it also puts your opponent in quite a bit of pain. It usually won't cause your opponent to tap, but it will often distract him long enough to secure a dominant grip.

1 Here my brother has secured a collar grip and I have secured a sleeve grip just above his elbow. Both of us are now fighting to get a grip with our other hand.

2 My brother beats me to the punch and secures a grip on my right sleeve. The damage has already been done, but to lessen his advantage, I reach my right hand over his arm to secure a sleeve grip on top. This will help control his arm and limit his ability to move me. It is important to note that if an opponent secures two grips and tries closing the distance, you should quickly grab him to take away some of his dominance, even if you don't lock onto him with the best grip.

3 Maintaining distance between my brother and I by locking my left arm, I push his left arm down with my right hand and lift my right knee. There are two things that need to be noticed here. First, in addition to pushing my right arm down, I have also brought it slightly back. This not only drops my brother's arm further toward the mat, but it also bends his wrist and weakens his grip. Second, I do not shoot my hips forward when I lift my knee. This would give my brother an opportunity to latch onto my leg and go for a single leg takedown. By keeping my hips back, I am lessening his chances of doing that. But you still have to be careful—if your opponent's grip doesn't break or he makes a move for a single leg, you want to quickly drop your leg back to the ground.

4 As I place my right knee down on my brother's wrist, I change my angle by turning my body slightly in a clockwise direction. The reason for this is because I want to apply downward pressure into his wrist rather than toward his body. The new angle also helps me press my knee up against my right arm, which locks everything in place and tweaks on his wrist. From here, I am going to drive my knee down while at the same time pulling my right shoulder up. It is very important that you don't pull up with just your hand—you want to get your whole shoulder into it to put the maximum amount of pressure on your opponent's wrist.

5 Having broken my brother's grip by driving down with my knee and up with my right shoulder, I now have a number of options at my disposal. I can execute a drop seoi-nage, jump into a triangle, or execute a flying armlock. With one simple technique, I have turned the tide of battle.

THROWS

One of my favorite things in this world is to land a perfect throw in a big competition. I love to hear the cheer of the crowd as I slam my opponent onto the mat, and I find pleasure in watching my opponent struggle back to his feet. Throws make judo exciting. I've had matches that were five seconds long. I walked out onto the mat, got a grip, threw my opponent squarely on his back, and walked away the victor.

Acquiring the skill to successfully execute throws in competition will require some dedication. Most of my students come from a jiu-jitsu background, and the first thing I tell them in judo practice is to check their jiu-jitsu training at the door. Those who take my advice usually excel the quickest. Instead of constantly trying to apply the judo techniques they pick up to their jiu-jitsu game, they learn judo as a separate discipline. By the time they reach the intermediate level in judo, combining the two arts comes naturally. They're suddenly applying the grip fighting skills they acquired while throwing directly to their groundwork. They're overwhelming their jiu-jitsu opponents with their newfound speed and power. And due to the dozens of hours they spent twisting and turning while practicing throws, their opponents have a much harder time holding them down. They become like a gymnast in tune with the martial arts, rolling into and out of submissions. I have little doubt that their progress would have been much more gradual if they had worn their jiu-jitsu eyeglasses during judo training.

Unfortunately learning how to throw involves getting thrown. I've been training judo for a long time, and never have I trained with someone who has allowed me to throw him fifty times a night without demanding the same in return. But there is more to getting thrown than just being fair to your training partner. It's virtually impossible to understand how to throw properly until you've been thrown yourself, much like it is hard to truly understand an armlock until you have been caught in one. Getting thrown teaches you how to escape a throw. It teaches you what you're doing wrong in your throws. Sometimes being a throwing dummy can actually benefit you more than the person doing the throwing.

In the beginning it is necessary that you go slow. An experienced judoka can throw someone with no martial arts experience ten feet into the air and have him land without injury. They can do this because they understand how the body needs to land to minimize the impact. A novice can't do that, which is why I stress the importance of taking it easy for the first few months. Practice your grips, practice your falls, and then practice each of the following throws several thousand times at the slowest possible speed. Only after you and your training partner are well versed on the basics should you start experimenting with speed and force.

FORWARD THROW MOVEMENT

When a student has trouble executing a forward throw, it's usually because he has improper form. And more often than not, the reason the student has bad form is because he hasn't practiced the basic forward throw movement enough. If you practice this drill for five minutes at the start of every judo session, you will develop the balance and footwork needed for every forward throw. Experienced jiu-jitsu practitioners might look at this drill and feel inclined to skip right to throws, but it is too important to pass up. It is the same as drilling an armlock—the more you do it, the better you will get.

To get started, you want to put two lines of tape on the mat about a foot and a half apart. For taller people, the tape should be a little farther apart, and for shorter people a little closer together. Both your feet and hands have tasks in this drill, but if you find it hard to keep track of both, start by keeping your arms at your sides and focusing on your footwork. However, it is important that you eventually bring your arms into the equation because a throw can't be done with your feet alone.

1 With my feet a shoulder's width apart and my toes lined up on the first line of tape, I reach forward and establish a grip on my imaginary opponent's gi.

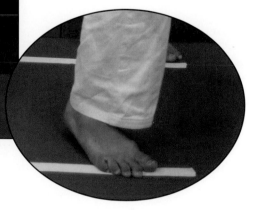

2 Because I have established an inside grip on my imaginary opponent, I lift his elbows with my arms, making him vulnerable to attack. At the same time, I step forward with my right foot, placing it in front of my left.

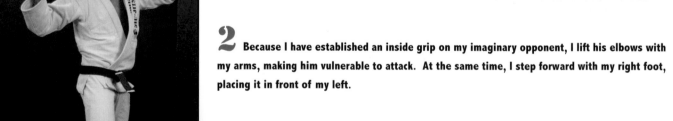

3 I step my left foot up to the line, placing it behind my right foot. Notice that my left foot is not flat, but rather up on its toes. To throw my imaginary opponent, I'm going to straighten my legs, rotate my hips in a counterclockwise direction, and tug on my opponent's gi with my left hand.

4 Having thrown my imaginary opponent by straightening my legs, rotating my hips in a counterclockwise direction, and pulling on my opponent's gi with my left hand, I am ready to start the forward throw movement in the opposite direction.

5 I start the drill over by lifting my arms and stepping my right foot forward.

6 I bring my left foot to the line, placing it behind my right foot.

7 I once again throw my imaginary opponent by straightening my legs, rotating my hips in a counterclockwise direction, and tugging on my opponent's gi with my left hand. I'm ready to start the drill over.

SEOI-NAGE

This is the first forward throw that I teach my new students. Once you get seoi-nage down, all the other forward throws should come naturally. The main difference will be how you grip your opponent.

1 Here I have a standard sleeve and collar grip. I am a few feet away from my brother, feet lined up with his, getting ready to turn in for the throw.

2 First I step forward with my right foot, placing it in front of my left. Next, I bring my left foot forward and place it behind my right. This is the exact same movement I made when executing the forward throw movement on the previous page. My right hand lets go of the collar because I only need one grip to execute a seoi-nage throw. Notice that my left grip is lifting my brother's right elbow, making him vulnerable on his right side. That opening allows me to slip in and rotate my body in a counterclockwise direction for the throw.

3 Having pivoted all the way around, I pull my brother's right arm tight across my chest with my left hand. I angle my right arm up and lock down my brother's right shoulder. I'm not grabbing his shoulder with my right hand, but rather making a fist and angling my wrist toward my head. From this position, I am ready to execute my throw. If my brother were to quickly drop his weight down, I would either abandon the move or drop down to my knees and throw from there. There are many ways to salvage this throw if things go wrong. However, if you're not familiar with this throw, it is beneficial to stop here, rotate back to the starting position, and then start over. This drill is called uchikomi, and it should be done over and over with every throw before you actually toss your opponent. It will help you develop the speed, technique, and precision needed for a good throw. You should start by doing ten uchikomi, and then having your partner do ten.

SPECIAL NOTE: Notice how in this photo my hips are lined up with my brother. Although in a judo match this is the best way to execute the technique, in jiu-jitsu competition it would possibly give my brother access to my back. To make this technique more applicable to jiu-jitsu competition, I would continue to rotate my hips in a counterclockwise direction so that my back was not directly against my brother's chest. By continuing to rotate, my right hip would turn out and my brother would get tossed onto his side. This eliminates his ability to get hooks in on my back.

4 Keeping my brother's shoulder locked with my right arm and pulling on his right sleeve with my left hand, I lift my brother with my hips and toss him to the mat.

5 To maintain control, I keep my left grip on my brother's sleeve and pull up. Anytime your opponent's arm is off the ground and extended, he is vulnerable. To gain even more control, I slide my right hand up my brother's arm and latch onto his sleeve just below my left hand. From here I can step my left leg over his head and fall right into an armbar. If my brother decides to roll up to his knees, I can take his back. If he rolls into me, I can keep his elbow controlled and drop into side control.

6 Continuing to pull up on my brother's arm to keep him from dropping his shoulder, I plant my right knee into his stomach for maximum control. I grab onto his collar with my right hand to help keep his shoulder off the mat and his arm vulnerable. This is the standard impact control position, and from here I have a number of options, many of which will be covered in the transitions section.

KOSHI-GURUMA

Once you have a good understanding of seoi-nage, you should be ready for koshi-guruma. It works great for no gi grappling and in MMA competition because instead of latching onto your opponent's collar, you're controlling his head with a really deep high grip. Even if you miss the throw, pulling guard is easy. Not that you'll have to do such a thing often; you have a tremendous amount of leverage with this throw, and it is very hard for your opponent to counter. You should consider this technique the bread and butter of your high grip throws. Get this one down, and other high grip throws such as harai-goshi and uchi-mata should fall right into place.

1 I have a standard sleeve and collar grip. I am a few feet away from my brother, feet lined up with his, getting ready to turn in for the throw.

2 I open my brother up on his right side by lifting his right elbow with my sleeve grip. I step in with my right foot to get my right hip as close to my brother as possible, and at the same time reach my right arm over his shoulder and around the back of his head.

3 Wrapping my right arm tightly around the back of my brother's head, I pull him close to me. At the same time, I step my left foot behind my right. This is setting my hips up for the throw. (If you have trouble with this, revisit the basic forward throw movement.) While doing all of this, I also pull my left arm in a counterclockwise direction, drawing my brother even closer to me. My whole goal is to make him a part of my body so that when I move, he moves. It is important to notice that I am not gripping with my right hand, which is the reason this move is so effective for MMA competition.

4 While continuing to pull up and around on my brother's gi with my left hand, I rotate my hips in a counterclockwise direction. Notice how my belt is slightly lower than my brother's belt, and how my right arm is moving his head in a counterclockwise direction, forcing him into a shoulder roll. It is also important to notice that my feet are toward the inside of his legs—you never want them to be on the outside. If they are, go back and practice forward throw movement until you have this down.

5 With my brother locked tight to my body, I lift his feet off the ground with my hips. I am basically doing a shoulder roll here, but because I have proper grips, I can make my brother land first. As always, I'm looking in the direction of the throw.

6 As my brother lands, I assume the standard impact control position by dropping my knee on his stomach. To keep his left side up and vulnerable, I continue to pull up on his sleeve with my left grip and latch onto his collar with my right. My legs are spread, giving me the ability to move quickly and take his back if he tries rolling up to his knees. The options from this position are covered in the transition section.

TAI-OTOSHI

Tai-otoshi is another forward throw that you'll be able to pull off in both jiu-jitsu and MMA competition. Instead of stepping in and getting snug tight with your opponent, you're going to stay on the outside. It requires less commitment, and it eliminates your opponent's ability to suplex you when your back is turned. This is the technique I used to throw Garth Taylor with when we were purple belts, and he outweighed me by a hundred pounds. To execute this move when no gi grappling you want to use an underhook instead of latching onto your opponent's collar.

1 I have established a pistol grip on my brother's left collar, and a sleeve grip on his right arm.

2 Instead of stepping toward my brother, I step to my right. I am still employing the standard forward throw movement—my right foot steps in front of my left, and then my left foot moves behind my right—but I have stepped to the outside rather than to the inside. As I do this, I pull on my brother's right sleeve with my left grip, making sure to employ both my arm and shoulder. At the same time, I push on his left side with my pistol grip and elbow. The success of the throw depends upon my ability to drive my brother's right elbow around me in a counterclockwise direction.

3 As I near the end of my rotation, I continue to pull my brother's right arm in a counterclockwise direction with my left sleeve grip, as well as push into his left side with my right pistol grip and elbow.

4 Still pulling on my brother's arm with my left hand and pushing into his body with my pistol grip and right elbow, I step my right foot out to the side, blocking him from stepping and reestablishing his balance and base. Notice that I have shoulder-to-shoulder contact on my right side.

5 As I continue to pull with my left hand and push with my right, my brother tries to step to reestablish his base but my right leg blocks him. As a result, he has no choice but to head into the throw.

6 Notice that I have not changed my grips. I'm still pulling up on my brother's sleeve with my left hand, keeping his arm exposed. I still have a pistol grip on his collar with my right hand, pushing down to keep him pinned to the mat. My feet are spread apart, ready for action. If my brother rolls away from me, I will release my left grip on his sleeve but keep my right grip on his collar. As he rolls, it will wrap me around him, giving me his back. If my brother rolls into me, I will trap his far arm and establish an armlock.

7 I drop my knee into my brother's stomach and assume the standard impact control position.

OSOTO-GARI

Osoto-gari is a very powerful leg throw. To execute this move in MMA or when grappling without a gi, you'll want to assume a koshi-guruma grip around your opponent's head instead of latching on with a high grip, but learning it the traditional way first is very important. It will give you a firm understanding of the fundamentals, which will make altering the move much easier.

1 My brother and I are facing off, searching for an opening. Notice that my left foot is forward and his right foot is forward. If we were boxing, my brother would be in a southpaw stance. This move only works when you and your opponent have opposite legs forward. If your opponent switches his stance, you can immediately transition to the osoto-gari variation, which is the next move in this section.

2 I have secured a sleeve grip on my brother's right arm just above his elbow. On his left side, I have secured a high grip with my thumb underneath his collar. I am going to attack his right leg, so if he steps his right leg back, I will abandon the throw.

3 Pushing off with my right leg, I step my left foot to the outside of my brother's right leg. As I take this step, I drive my right arm in a counterclockwise direction to push his head toward my left foot. I also pull downward in a counterclockwise direction with my right hand and shoulder, which drops my brother's right elbow, destroys his base, and makes him vulnerable on his right side. Notice that I have stepped all the way in for full body contact. We are chest to chest.

4 Because I have continued to rotate my brother's body in a counterclockwise direction using my arms, his base has weakened significantly and the majority of is weight has come down on his right leg, which is exactly what I want. Here I am kicking my right leg through the small gab between our feet. My leg has a slight bend, and my toes are pointed straight. If you are new to this technique, this is where you should stop. Instead of kicking out your partner's leg, transition back to the starting position and practice the moves up to this point again and again. Drilling a move uchikomi will pay off big time in the long run, as well as limit injuries to both you and your partner.

5 Continuing with my upper body counterclockwise rotation, my brother is starting to lean back. To completely destroy his base, I kick my leg forcibly back into his right leg. When doing this move, imagine that there is a soccer ball behind you and then try to kick it as far as possible with your heel. You want to drive your leg through your opponent's leg and up toward the ceiling.

6 With my brother's leg hooked, I continue to drive my right hand and shoulder down as if I were trying to punch the mat. I am also still pulling on his right elbow with my left hand. You want to keep the circular rotation up to the very end to generate more force behind your throw, as well as to ensure that your opponent's upper back and head hit the canvas before you do.

7 Keeping my brother's right leg up with my right leg, I drive my right shoulder to the ground to get the most impact out of the throw. You have to be very careful with this technique. My brother knows to keep his chin tucked to his chest upon impact, but if you get into a scuffle in the street, the chances are your assailant won't. Because it is so easy to drive your opponent's head into the ground with this move, you should never do it on the street.

8 I immediately drop my knee down to my brother's stomach and assume the standard impact control position. From here I am going to transition right to a submission without letting go of my grips, which we will cover in the transitions section.

OSOTO-GARI VARIATION

When both you and your opponent are standing with the same leg forward, it is impossible to execute the standard osoto-gari. In such a situation you can either switch your stance or utilize the osoto-gari variation. The variation of osoto-gari tends to work better for jiu-jitsu competition because it doesn't require full body contact. It also works great on opponents who maintain distance and keep their body stiff, which happens to be two common traits of strict jiu-jitsu practitioners. And because you are going to hang on the outside, hopping into your opponent only when you are ready to commit to the throw, your opponent will have fewer opportunities to counter your movement. However, this technique doesn't work as well as the standard osoto-gari for MMA because the distance you maintain gives your opponent an opportunity to punch. In MMA, you generally want to be in or out.

1 My brother and I are squared off, searching for an opening. He has chosen to bend over slightly and assume more of a jiu-jitsu stance. Because we have opposite legs forward, I am looking to apply the standard ouchi-gari.

2 My brother steps in to engage and I assume a sleeve and collar grip. Because we now have the same leg forward, I can no longer attempt the standard osoto-gari. However, I am now open to apply the osoto-gari variation.

3 I kick my right leg past my brother's right leg, and then chop my heel into the back of his knee. I will continue to dig my heel in to break down his base. With my upper body I am doing everything I did in the previous technique—pushing his head down toward my right foot and pulling his right arm toward me in a counterclockwise direction—but now I am locking my right arm straight to maintain distance between our bodies. This is where I will decide if I will go through with the throw. If I can't break his base, then I will abort. If he maintains his base and I don't abort, then he has the ability to throw me with the same technique.

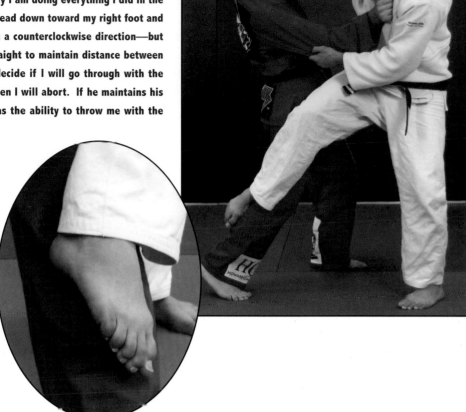

4 Feeling my brother's base weaken, I decide to go through with the throw. Continuing to turn his body in a counterclockwise direction with my arms, I slide my right leg deeper behind his right knee. In order not to get too spread out, I hop forward on my left foot.

5 Having broken my brother's base, I can afford to have a little more body contact and hop further in, putting me more to the side. To slam him to the mat, all it takes is a little pressure from my right leg and continued counterclockwise rotation with my upper body. Deciding how many hops to take depends upon how close you are to your opponent. Sometimes it takes one, and sometimes it takes three. The important part is breaking down your opponent's base before you come forward to engage.

6 Keeping my brother's right leg up with my right leg, I drive my right shoulder to the ground to get the most impact out of the throw.

7 I immediately plant my knee into my brother's stomach to assume the standard impact control position. From here I am going to transition right to a submission without letting go of my grips.

OUCHI-GARI

Ouchi-gari is an excellent throw for MMA competition because unlike the single or double leg takedowns, it requires very little energy to execute. If you are successful with the throw, you'll usually land in full guard, ready to pound on your opponent. I use this technique all the time in competition, and it has been extremely effective. I did a variation of this technique where I picked my opponent's right leg up with my right leg, and then I picked up his left leg with my hand. I drove him down into the mat, and fifteen minutes later an ambulance came to the competition to pick him up. It is a very explosive move that can end the fight in a split second.

1 I have secured a sleeve grip on my brother's right arm with my left hand, and pistol grip on his left collar. Notice that I am in a southpaw stance, making it so that we have opposite legs forward. If my brother were to switch his feet, I would not be able to go for this throw.

2 I take a step forward with my right foot. My right elbow is locked to my brother's body, and I'm pulling his left arm into me with my sleeve grip.

3 Following the basic forward throw movement, my left foot comes forward and plants behind my right, getting me even closer to my brother's body. Based on my positioning, my brother expects me to rotate my body in a counterclockwise direction and execute a standard forward throw.

4 Because I am going to rotate my body in a clockwise direction and push my brother backwards, I shoot my right leg behind my brother's left leg, hindering him from stepping back and reestablishing his base.

5 Throwing my right leg back, I sweep my brother's left foot off the mat. At the same time, I rotate my upper body in a clockwise direction toward the foot that I swept. I will continue both motions until my brother lands, rotating in as much of a circle as possible.

6 As my brother lands, I drive my right shoulder toward the ground to generate as much force as possible. My right knee comes down over his left leg. From here, I will keep his left leg planted with my right leg as I move my left leg in a counterclockwise direction so I can pass his guard and assume side control. Notice that neither of my grips change. I still have the standard sleeve and collar grip, which I will use to transition into a submission. Trying to reposition your hands will give your opponent an opportunity to escape or attack.

KOUCHI-GARI

Kouchi-Gari is the younger brother of ouchi-gari; they work great with one another, and you can transition back and forth between them until you land one. The technique requires that you kick one of your opponent's legs out from underneath him, so you can use it to set up a really deep single leg takedown. Timing is crucial, but once you get that down you'll be a dangerous force. I used technique and a handful of others so often in jiu-jitsu competition that pretty soon my opponents wanted nothing to do with my stand-up. The second a match started, they instantly pulled guard.

1 Notice that my brother and I both have our left leg forward. If we had opposite legs forward, this technique wouldn't apply. Here I have a standard sleeve and collar grip.

2 To set up the technique, I take a step back with my left foot. As I do this, I rotate my body in a counterclockwise direction and pull my brother's right shoulder forward using my grip on his sleeve. To maintain his base, my brother takes a step forward with his right foot.

3 Not comfortable with the new position, my brother steps back to our original position, and I follow by bringing my left foot forward again. From here I am going to repeat the process—step my left foot back, rotate my body in a counterclockwise direction, and pull on his right sleeve. Feeling comfortable because nothing happened the first time, my brother will step forward and fall into the trap.

4 Having stepped my left foot back, my brother steps his right foot forward. Before his foot touches down, I sweep my right foot forward and catch it. Because his right side base has been eliminated, I drive his body downward by pulling his sleeve in a counterclockwise direction and pushing the left side of his body toward my right foot with my pistol grip. At the same time, I use my right foot to kick his right leg in the direction his toes are pointing.

5 As my brother falls, I drive my right shoulder toward the ground to maximize the force behind the throw. Notice here that I have not dropped my right knee to the canvas, but rather positioned it over my brother's right leg. If I dropped it to the mat, my brother would have me in the guard position and be open to attack.

6 As I lower my body, my knee penetrates my brother's guard. I have maintained my original grips. Because I am pulling up on my brother's left arm with my sleeve grip, he cannot maneuver around and take my back. My right hand continues to push down and hold him in place. From here, I will keep his right leg trapped with my knee and jump my left leg over his right leg to assume the side control position.

OUCHI-GARI TO UCHI-MATA

Jiu-jitsu practitioners tend to stand more bent over than judo players. When you try to execute an uchi-mata on an opponent in such a low stance, he can easily counter your throw by latching onto your leg. Utilizing a combination is a great way to solve this problem. If you start off with an ouchi-gari, you'll not only force your opponent into a higher stance, but also confuse him with your body movement, which tells him that you're attempting a backward throw. As he prepares to defend the backward throw, you quickly switch to uchi-mata, which is a forward throw. Anytime you start with one technique and end with another, it makes it much harder for your opponent to counter. In jiu-jitsu and judo you never want to be one-dimensional. You want to throw your opponent off as much as possible, and combinations are an excellent way to do that. This particular technique works great for MMA while tied up in the clinch against the fence. You start with a really deep ouchi-gari, it is not working for whatever reason, and then you hop, hop, hop right into uchi-mata.

1 My brother and I are squared off. He has chosen a bent over jiu-jitsu stance, making it difficult for me to attempt an uchi-mata throw.

2 My brother steps forward to engage, making it so that we both have our right foot forward. In my mind I am already thinking of using ouchi-gari to set up uchi-mata, so I establish a sleeve grip on his right arm and a high grip on his left side.

3 I step my right foot in front of my left, and then place my left foot behind my right. If you have trouble with this, revisit standard forward throw movement. If I was going to commit to the ouchi-gari, then I would pull with my right hand and push with my left to break my brother's base, but I don't want to do that. This is more for show, to get my brother to react to a move I am shortly going to abandon.

4 As I trap my brother's left leg, he becomes certain that I'm going for ouchi-gari and prepares to defend a backward throw. If he had time to think, he would realize that my upper body is not following through with the ouchi-gari movement. Instead of rotating my body in a clockwise direction for the backwards throw, I am rotating my body in a counterclockwise direction. So I am pulling with my left grip and pushing with my right. If you are trying to apply this move in MMA competition, then you should use over-hooks or under-hooks to control your opponent.

5 Quickly hopping once on my left foot and turning my body in a counterclockwise direction, I transition into a full-fledged uchi-mata. Notice that I am stiff-arming my brother to keep distance between us, much like I did in tai-otoshi. I have also shifted my focus from my right side to my left, which is the direction that I will throw. The move comes extremely easy because my brother never saw it coming.

6 Hoping on my left foot again in a counterclockwise direction, my right hand sweeps in the same direction, almost like an overhand punch. I continue to pull on my brother's right sleeve to further break his base.

7 I have finished hopping and my left foot plants firmly on the ground. I shoot my right leg toward the ceiling to stop my brother from being able to hang on through the throw. Continuing to turn in a counterclockwise direction, his body goes over.

8 The moment my brother lands, I drive my weight forward to close the distance between us. If you are slow to cover that distance, your opponent will most likely pull you into his guard.

9 Maintaining my original grips, I drive my right elbow deep into my brother's chest to keep him from moving around and taking my back. I use my left grip to pull up on his sleeve and keep his right arm off the ground and exposed. It is very hard for my brother to move in this position, making it easy for me to transition into a submission.

FOOT-SWEEP

Foot sweeps are magical because with just one small movement you can send your opponent flying through the air. Unlike the majority of other throws, sweeps can be executed successfully without gripping your opponent, which makes them excellent for all competition, including jiu-jitsu, judo, and MMA. The reason you don't see a plethora of foot sweeps in competition is because they require impeccable timing and cat-like speed. The dedication needed to develop dangerous foot sweeps turns many students off, but those who put in the time will eventually excel. One of my jiu-jitsu white belts recently dominated a competition with foot sweeps. He executed one on his first opponent, landed in side control, and then instantly transitioned to an armlock. In his next match, he did the exact same thing. This came out of a guy who had trained for just a few months, so foot-sweep techniques are certainly within everyone's reach.

1 My brother and I both have a standard sleeve and collar grip.

2 Trying to bait my brother into a foot sweep, I step to my left side with my left foot and use my grips to pull my brother's body in the same direction. Not wanting me to find an opening, he mimics my movement by stepping his right foot to his right. If we were dancing, I would be the one leading, which is key.

3 To keep from getting too spread out, I bring my right foot toward my left. Still mimicking my movement, my brother does the same. I could have attempted the foot sweep here, but I want my brother to get comfortable with our movement so his defenses drop.

4 Again I take a step with my left foot, pulling my brother along. He matches by stepping with his right foot.

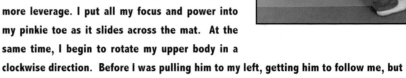

5 As my brother lifts his left foot to bring it closer to his right, I catch his foot with my right foot. Notice that I have angled my foot so that my big toe is up in the air and my pinky toe is scrapping along the mat. This allows me to place the bottom of my foot against my brother's leg for more leverage. I put all my focus and power into my pinkie toe as it slides across the mat. At the same time, I begin to rotate my upper body in a clockwise direction. Before I was pulling him to my left, getting him to follow me, but now I am going to force his body in a circular motion in the opposite direction.

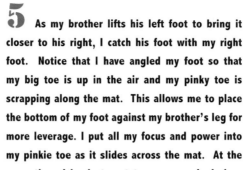

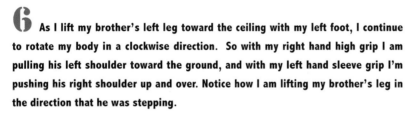

6 As I lift my brother's left leg toward the ceiling with my left foot, I continue to rotate my body in a clockwise direction. So with my right hand high grip I am pulling his left shoulder toward the ground, and with my left hand sleeve grip I'm pushing his right shoulder up and over. Notice how I am lifting my brother's leg in the direction that he was stepping.

7 In this photo I have planted my left knee on my brother's stomach to assume the standard impact control position. This position allows me to easily transition into submissions, but it took some work to get here. Because sweeps are kind of funky, I first landed with my right knee in my brother's stomach. It doesn't take much effort to make the switch, but you must be careful. If your opponent quickly recovers from the sweep and tries to pull you into his guard, it is best to obtain side control before shifting the position of your knees.

SWITCH FOOT-SWEEP

This is the exact move I used to win the gold medal at the 1999 Canadian Open. My opponent was ranked number three in the US at the time, and I was ranked number two. He was undoubtedly one of the best judoka out there when we paired up, but I tossed him with this throw in less than ten seconds and ended the match. What makes this throw so effective is you get your opponent thinking you're going one way, and then you go another. It is called the 'switch foot sweep' because you're actually changing directions in mid-air, making it an extremely unorthodox move. It requires baiting your opponent, and it works beautifully in judo and jiu-jitsu competition because your opponent will usually take the bait. It doesn't work as well for MMA because in an anything-goes environment fighters tend to be more cautious.

1 My brother and I are squared off, searching for an opening. Because we have the same leg forward, I am open for the switch foot sweep.

2 I have secured a standard sleeve and high grip. Notice how I have already turned my hips slightly in a counterclockwise direction. This will set me up for the foot sweep.

3 Keeping distance between us, I turn in with the standard forward throw movement. My brother instantly suspects that I am going to execute a forward throw, which is what I want. I am baiting him here, trying to get him to defend.

4 Pulling my brother's right side close to me with my sleeve grip, he suspects that I am going for a standard uchi-mata or harai-goshi. He falls into the trap by thrusting his left hip forward, which is the standard defense for a forward throw. Notice that he is extreme left and I am extreme right, and that our hips are touching. It would be very hard for me to execute a forward throw from this position.

5 Abandoning the forward throw, I sneak my right leg behind my brother's left leg. The transition is easy because my brother is currently defending a forward throw.

6 Rotating my body in a clockwise direction, I trust my right leg behind both of my brother's knees. It can be done by tapping just one of your opponent's legs, but catching both works much better. I use my right grip to pull my brother's collar toward the ground, and I use my left grip to push his elbow up and around, further driving his body downwards.

7 As you can see in the photo, there is plenty of force behind this throw. The hard impact makes it difficult for your opponent to pull you into his guard when the fight first hits the ground. Any time you rattle your opponent, you have a better shot at transitioning right into a submission.

8 My brother managed to break his fall well and keep his wits, so instead of transitioning to the standard impact control position, I use a modified side control position off my landing. I drop my left hand down to his hip to stop him from rotating and putting me into his guard. I still have a high grip with my right hand, and I use it to pull my hips into his left shoulder, locking his body to the ground. Remember, rarely do you want to switch your grips when you hit the ground. It takes too much time and gives your opponent a greater chance to pull guard.

MESHING TECHNIQUES

If you've studied and practiced the techniques in this book sequentially, then you should have an understanding of basic judo. You have spent hours grip fighting with your training partners, and you have executed hundreds of forward throws, backward throws, and combinations that utilize both. So far you have trained judo with your judo eyeglasses on, meaning you have learned each technique without worrying about how it will apply to your jiu-jitsu game. Now it is time to put your jiu-jitsu eyeglasses back on, take what you have learned in judo, and combine the two disciplines. In this section we are going to learn how to deal with your jiu-jitsu opponent's counters to your judo throws. We will work on taking your jiu-jitsu opponent out of his game plan by utilizing judo techniques. It is time to take your judo and apply it to a match that has jiu-jitsu rules. After spending an ample amount of time with the following techniques, I think you will be pleasantly surprised with the improvements to your game.

FORCING HIGH STANCE

Many jiu-jitsu practitioners rely heavily upon wrestling techniques for takedowns because they don't have a good understanding of grip fighting or throws. As a result, they often assume a low, bent over stance because it allows them to shoot in for a single or double leg takedown. Although it is still possible to throw an opponent who is bent over, a better approach is to first force your opponent into a high stance using this technique. Having been lifted out of his comfort zone, your opponent will usually focus on dropping back down to an elevation he feels comfortable with. Before he has a chance to do that, however, you're going to introduce him to a throw.

1 Here my brother and I are pretending to be in a jiu-jitsu tournament. Although my goal will be to throw him, I assume the standard low jiu-jitsu stance. If I came at him in a high stance, he might recognize that I know judo, become wary of throws, and immediately pull guard. Right now he thinks he is up against a fellow jiu-jitsu practitioner, which makes him feel comfortable with engaging.

2 We come forward and begin fighting for grips. In judo, grip fighting is extremely explosive and fast, but in jiu-jitsu it is generally much slower, especially in the white, blue, and purple belt divisions. So here we are just playing around, searching for something. Notice that I have already controlled my brother's right elbow with a sleeve grip.

3 I catch my brother off guard by transitioning from slow jiu-jitsu speed to fast judo speed. As I step in with my right foot, I pull my brother's right arm in close to me with my left grip and shoot my right hand underneath his left arm. My combined movement brings us chest to chest. Continuing to drive forward with my left leg, leading with my hips, forces my brother into a high stance. Since my brother is pretending to be a strict jiu-jitsu practitioner, he is currently out of his comfort zone.

4 Wasting no time, I immediately place my left foot behind my right and rotate into an under-hook version of koshi-guruma. Just as before, I use my left arm to pull my brother's sleeve in a counterclockwise direction, and I use my right arm to drive his upper-body into the throw. This move is especially good for jiu-jitsu because it doesn't land me in a head and arm position, which would give my brother access to my back. You can also use the under-hook with uchi-mata or a drop down tai-otoshi. The important part here is to lift your opponent up to a standing position, making your throws much harder to counter.

5 Having successfully stood my brother up, I move right into the throw.

OVER-HOOK HARAI-GOSHI

A lot of times you can use the slow moving pace of jiu-jitsu matches to get unorthodox grips that are hard to come by in a judo match. The over-hook harai-goshi is a perfect example. I've found it difficult to successfully execute this technique in judo because my opponents usually move too fast to establish the over-hook, but I land it all the time against slower moving jiu-jitsu practitioners. It shows how judo can improve your jiu-jitsu and give you a leg up in competition.

1 I've latched onto my brother with the standard sleeve and collar grip.

2 My brother tries to reach his left arm underneath my right arm to establish an under-hook, which is a move strict jiu-jitsu practitioners go for all the time. Some are even quite successful at establishing the under-hook, but it's not because the move is hard to counter. They're successful because most of their opponents are also jiu-jitsu practitioners who have little grip fighting experience. This move is actually tremendously easy to counter with the proper knowledge.

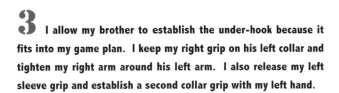

3 I allow my brother to establish the under-hook because it fits into my game plan. I keep my right grip on his left collar and tighten my right arm around his left arm. I also release my left sleeve grip and establish a second collar grip with my left hand.

4 I use my left hand to feed the right collar of my brother's gi into my right hand, giving me a better grip and locking his left arm tight under my right arm. It is now very hard for him to free his arm. If he attempts to pull away, I can move right into a flying triangle, which you will learn about in the last section of the book.

5 After feeding the right side of my brother's collar into my right hand, I drop my left hand down and reestablish a grip on his sleeve. At the same time, I step my right foot between my brother's legs to set up the throw.

6 I bring my left foot behind my right foot and begin to rotate my body in a counterclockwise direction. I use my left grip to pull my brother's right arm in the same direction. It is important to notice how I have brought my left wrist close to my face, almost as if I am checking the time on a watch. My right hip is deep inside, and I maintain a tight over-hook on my brother's left arm by continuing to latch onto his collar with my right hand.

7 Rotating my hips in a counterclockwise direction and twisting my brother's body using both grips, I thrust my right leg in front of my brother's right leg to keep him from taking a step and reestablishing his base and balance.

8 As we land, I keep my right knee tight to my brother's body to maintain control and keep him from using the momentum of the throw to roll me over to my back. My left leg is posted back to establish base and balance. Notice that I have not switched my grips.

9 Still gripping my brother's collar with my right hand, I let go of my left sleeve grip. I drop my left hand down and use it to assume a collar grip above my right hand. For this grip, I wrap my fingers around his collar and keep my thumb on the outside. As I drive my left hand down, tightening my brother's collar around his neck, I drop my left forearm into his throat to complete the choke. As you can see, my brother is tapping out with his right hand.

GRIPPING THROW

If you train judo at least once a week for a couple of months, your grip fighting will improve. This is an excellent technique to utilize against an opponent who hasn't spent as much time developing his grips. While he is focused on fighting and defending your superior grips, you'll be setting up your throw.

1 My brother and I are in a low jiu-jitsu stance, searching for an opening.

2 We both assume a sleeve and collar grip. Neither one of us have an advantage over the other. However, for this move we are going to pretend that my brother doesn't know any judo. Coming from jiu-jitsu, he is about to be overwhelmed by my judo grips.

3 Still gripping my brother's collar with my right hand, I drive my right elbow to the ground. At the same time, I use my sleeve grip to drive his right arm down. I am forcing him into an even lower stance, hoping for a reaction so I can counter. If you desire to learn this move without a gi, then you should drive your opponent's head down by cupping the back of his neck with your right hand.

4 My brother resists my attempt to pull him into a low stance by standing up, which is the reaction I was hoping for. I don't attempt to stop him from doing this.

5 While my brother is focused on resisting and defending my grips, I step my left foot to the outside of his right leg, changing my angle. I let up on downward pressure, making him believe that I have abandoned whatever I was working on.

6 By taking my step to the side, I have now set up my body for a clockwise rotation. As I start to turn, I again force my brother's right collar to the ground using my right grip, except this time I put downward pressure in the same clockwise direction that my body is turning. I apply additional downward pressure with my sleeve grip, but because I want his body to turn in a clockwise direction, I use little strength. Notice that I have dropped into a squat position to help drop my brother's body.

7 Notice that my feet haven't changed their position on the ground from the last photo. I have rotated my body, but my feet stay in the same locations. My brother goes down not because I am tripping him, but rather because he can't keep up with the downward spiral my arms and hips have cast him in. As he starts to go down, I continue with my rotation and he looses his ability to stay on his feet. Notice that he has a lot of momentum here. You don't want to do this technique slow. It should be done with a quick jerking motion of your grips.

8 I land right in the standard impact control position with my knee on my brother's stomach. My left hand is still controlling his sleeve, and my right hand is still controlling his collar. I do not change my grips.

ASHI-BARAI

If your opponent assumes a low jiu-jitsu stance, it can be difficult to chuck him with a standard forward throw because he can counter by latching onto your legs with his arms or simply dropping down to his knees. Utilizing ashi-barai on an opponent in a low stance will lessen your risk of getting caught and pulled into his comfort zone. It's a tricky technique to counter because it looks like you're executing a backward throw like osoto-gari in the beginning, but then you quickly turn the opposite way and launch your opponent with a forward throw. When done with enough speed, you almost always catch your opponent off guard.

1 My brother assumes a low jiu-jitsu stance, and I do the same to hide the fact that I'm trained in judo throws.

2 I come in very aggressive and establish a sleeve grip above my brother's right elbow and a high collar grip with my right hand.

3 Pulling on my brother's sleeve, I step my right foot explosively toward the outside of my brother's right leg. Right now it looks like I will attack my brother's right side with a harai-goshi or an osoto-gari.

4 Stepping my left foot to the outside of my brother's right leg, I turn my body in a clockwise direction. This leads my brother to believe that I'm attempting to execute a backwards throw, so his first instinct is to turn his body in a clockwise direction to stop me from getting one of my legs behind him.

5 Having rotated in a clockwise direction, I lift my right foot and plant it just below my brother's left knee. Notice that my big toe is up and my little toe is down; this allows me to place the bottom of my foot on my brother's shin and cover as much surface area as possible. With my brother's leg trapped, I use my high grip and clockwise rotation to pull his body downward. As his body falls forward, he tries to take a step to regain his base and balance, but my foot bars him from doing so.

6 My brother looses his balance and his right foot comes off the ground. Notice how I am looking in the direction that I'm throwing.

7 My brother has no choice but to head into the throw. Because I executed this move with speed and power, his body generates a lot of momentum.

8 Although this throw lands me in somewhat of an awkward position, I do not change my grips. I use my sleeve and collar grips to pin my brother to the mat and limit his movement. My right leg has come straight to the ground, giving me side control. If I tried to plant my right foot in a better position, my brother might do some maneuvering and pull me into his guard.

9 Because my brother isn't putting up a fight or trying and pull me into his guard, I make a quick switch to the standard impact control position. If he had put up a struggle, I would have stayed where I was and lowered my body to achieve a more secure side control.

ASHI-BARAI PICKUP

Usually you'll get the throw that you want about twenty percent of the time. Because of this, you want to have as many combinations as possible packed into your arsenal. If you go for a throw and your opponent counters, you should move right into a second throw. If your opponent counters your second throw, you should move into a third. Persistence is key. This particular technique works great when your opponent counters the standard ashi-barai by stepping over your leg. While he is congratulating himself on escaping your first throw attempt, you're using his counter to transition directly into another one.

1 Here I am executing the standard ashi-barai by stepping to the outside, trapping my brother's left leg, and pulling his body downward in a clockwise direction with a high grip.

2 My brother reads my movement and steps his left leg over my right foot. Now that he can plant his foot in front of him and reestablish his base and balance, I quickly abandon the throw.

3 As my brother plants his left foot down, he is still in a vulnerable position. To capitalize on that opportunity, I decide to immediately transition into another throw.

4 I plant my right foot behind my left, setting me up for another throw.

5 As I drop and pivot my body in a clockwise direction, I step my left foot up to my brother's left foot. Notice that I have brought my left hip in close to his body, which is key for generating power and leverage for the throw. I've positioned my body into a launch position with my feet somewhat close together. I release my left sleeve grip and reach down and wrap my left hand tightly around the inside of my brother's right thigh. My right hand is still controlling his collar.

6 I use my right high grip to lift up on my brother's collar and pull his upper body in a clockwise direction. This, in combination with my left hand, helps create lift. I still have body-to-body contact.

7 With my left hand still wrapped around the inside of my brother's right leg, I push off with my legs, turn my body in a clockwise direction, and lift my brother off the mat. Notice that I am thrusting my left hip into my brother, and that I am still using my right hand to lift up on his collar in a clockwise direction.

8 Still rotating in a clockwise direction and thrusting into my brother with my left hip, my left foot comes off the ground. Here I am balancing on one leg, continuing to drive him over into the throw. I have a lot of control over how my brother lands. If I wish, I could stop my throw short and pile-drive his head into the mat. When I was a blue belt, I won Joe Moreira's tournament with this throw. My opponent landed so hard it gave me an opportunity to immediately transition to a submission and tap him out.

9 I decide to follow through with my throw instead of dropping my brother down onto his head. If you are going up against an opponent who has basic knowledge of throws, then this is generally what you want to do. If you go into the throw with half speed hoping to drive your opponent's head into the mat, you might not get the throw at all. It is best to always close the deal. Notice that I am still controlling my brother's right leg with my left hand, and I'm bringing my weight down on top of him. You don't want any separation on this one because it will give your opponent a chance to pull you into his guard.

10 As I land, I drive my weight into my brother so there is no separation between us. My left knee is tight against his left leg to keep him from pulling me into his guard. I pull up with my grip on his right leg to keep everything tight. My right grip is still on his collar, pinning him to the mat. My right knee is on his left arm to immobilize it. It is important to quickly secure everything after a throw because your opponent will most likely try to scramble for position. If everything is done right, you shouldn't have to pass guard. You'll land in side control, ready to use your original grips to transition into a submission.

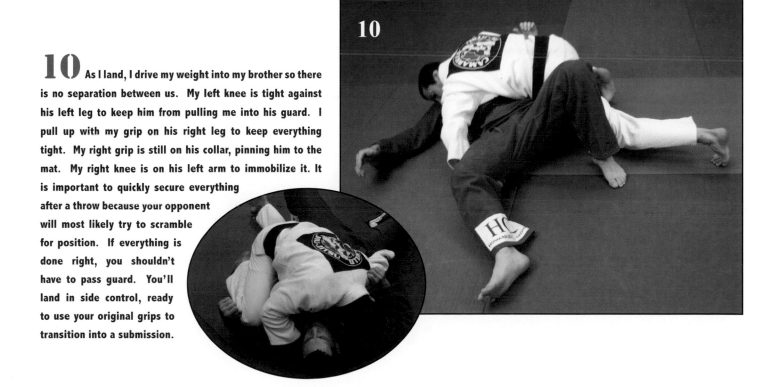

BELT GRIP TAI-OTOSHI

This is a variation of the standard tai-otoshi designed specifically for jiu-jitsu competition. It allows you to execute the throw from the outside, which hinders your opponent from latching onto your leg and countering the throw. This technique put me on the map when I used it to chuck Garth Taylor in the absolute division at the Copa Pacifica in '98. Most jiu-jitsu practitioners won't see this throw coming until it's too late.

1 My brother and I have both assumed low jiu-jitsu stances. I already have the belt grip tai-otoshi in mind, so the second we are within range, I am going to jump in, get a high grip, and go.

2 I establish a sleeve grip above my brother's right elbow with my left hand, and then I lunge my right foot toward the outside of my brother's left foot and drive my right arm over his back, almost like I'm throwing an overhand right.

3 Reaching deep over my brother's back, I latch onto his belt with my right hand. Now I am set up for the throw.

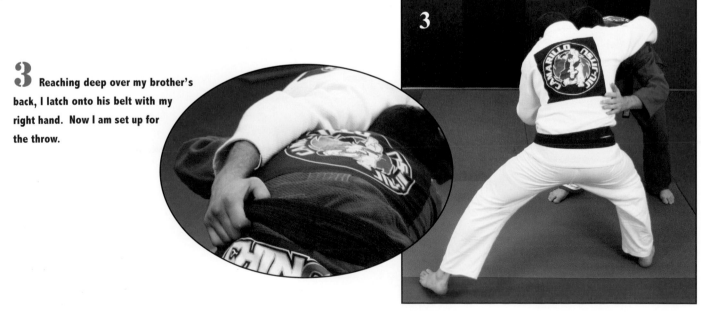

4 As I pivot in a counterclockwise direction on my right foot, I step my left foot behind my right. At the same time, I use my sleeve grip to pull my brother's right arm in a counterclockwise direction, and I use my belt grip to pull his upper body in a counterclockwise direction.

5 Planting my weight on my left foot, I shoot my right leg out to trap my brother's right leg. I continue to rotate in a counterclockwise direction, using my grips to pull my brother's sleeve and upper body in the same direction.

6 With my brother's right leg trapped, he can't take a step forward to reestablish his balance and base. As I continue to rotate my body in a counterclockwise direction, I drop my right shoulder toward my left foot. I haven't stopped pulling on my brother's sleeve or belt. Notice how I am looking in the direction of the throw and exaggerating my movement. This will help guarantee success with the technique.

7 As my brother lands, I can let my body come down on top of his, potentially knocking the air out of him. In this photo, however, I elect to stay on my feet so I can drop my knee into his stomach and assume the standard impact control position.

8 I plant my right knee into my brother's stomach. Notice that I haven't changed my grips. The reason that my right hand is now at my brother's side is because I've pulled so hard on his belt that it has slipped to this position. Now the harder I pull up on his belt, the deeper my knee will dig into his gut. I am still controlling his sleeve with my left hand. My left leg is back for balance and mobility. From here I will transition to a submission.

TANI-OTOSHI

When you enter jiu-jitsu competition, it will work to your advantage to hide the fact that you have judo training. If you go out there and start grabbing and moving, grabbing and moving, completely dominating your opponent in grip fighting, you'll probably scare him into jumping guard. A much better approach is to go out there and play the normal jiu-jitsu 'touchy-feely' game. Believing his grips are as strong as yours, your opponent will start to feel comfortable. Then once you've established a grip that you like, you explode into a move like tani-otoshi, catching him completely off guard. Tani-otoshi is launched off a funky under-hook on your opponent's leg, and it is very deceiving because it's difficult for your opponent to tell what you're trying to achieve. By the time he figures it out, his feet will already be off the ground.

1 My brother and I are in a low jiu-jitsu stance, searching for an opening. Here I have my poker face on. I'm playing a slow jiu-jitsu game rather than a fast judo game because I don't want to alert him to the fact that I have throws in my arsenal. If he smells something funny, he might pull guard.

2 My brother reaches out in typical slow jiu-jitsu fashion and establishes a collar grip, and I latch onto his sleeve with both hands as if I am going to try to break his grip. This is standard practice, and he doesn't sense anything strange going on. He has no idea that I am setting my left hand up to make a transition.

3 This is where the move gets explosive. I use my right grip on my brother's sleeve to pull his right arm in close to my body. As I do this, I slip my left hand around the inside of his right arm and then reach toward the back of his right leg. I am moving my upper body toward his legs as I do this.

4 I step my left foot behind my brother's right foot and cup my left hand around the inside of his right thigh. My brother is pretty much locked in here. I have maintained control of his right arm with my right sleeve grip, keeping it tight to my body. My left leg is stopping him from stepping his right foot back.

5 With everything in place, I move my right foot in a clockwise direction and plant it down on the outside of my brother's right leg. I am trying to get behind him as much as possible for the throw.

6 Now that my feet are in position, I drive my hips forward to start the throw. I am also driving down on his right arm with my sleeve grip to further break his base. Notice how this is starting to collapse him backwards.

7 Continuing to drive my hips forward, I start to collapse backwards. My brother's first instinct is to turn into me, but because I have such tight control on his right arm with my sleeve grip, he will have no choice but to land on his back.

8 My brother lands first, and then I land shortly thereafter. Notice that my hips are in the air because I am still driving, and that I have maintained my original grips upon impact. Although I haven't come all the way down yet, I'm already driving my head into my brother's right shoulder. I'm going to use my head in conjuncture with my grips to make a quick transition to side control.

9 To keep my brother from rolling into me and putting me in his guard, I drive with my hips and pull with my arms to get my head up onto his chest. Once there, I drive my head and left shoulder down to keep my brother pinned.

10 As I continue to roll and assume the side control position, I release my left grip on my brother's leg and wrap it around the back of his neck for head control. Only after I feel comfortable will I release my right sleeve grip and establish proper hand positioning. Notice here how I am pushing off with my feet to drive my body into my brother. This will further hinder him from scrambling and possibly trapping me in his guard.

STOPPING WRESTLING SHOT

Because jiu-jitsu doesn't have exceptional takedowns, many jiu-jitsu practitioners learn wrestling techniques to get their opponents to the mat. The single and double leg takedowns are the most common. Sprawling is an excellent way to counter the single and double leg, but now that you possess solid grip fighting skills, you have other options. I've spent a lot of time developing ways to grip your opponent's gi to stop him cold in his tracks when he shoots in. This first technique is used for a double leg takedown. It will land you in a more commanding position than the traditional sprawl, and it should improve your standing game phenomenally.

1 My brother and I have assumed a low wrestling/jiu-jitsu stance.

2 The moment I see my brother shoot in for a double leg takedown, I latch onto both of his collars with my hands and straighten my arms.

3 Now that I have established my grips on my brother's collar, I use those grips to drive my brother down as I sprawl my legs back.

4 By dropping my weight down on top of my brother and pinning his collar to the mat with both hands, I have stopped my brother's shot. Notice that I am up on my toes. My legs are relaxed here so that if my brother continues to drive forward, I will slide backwards on my feet. I don't try to hold my ground. If he wants to waste energy and push forward, I will go with it. Once he has stopped driving, I can then use my grips on his collar to help make the transition to his back.

FINDING BALANCE ON A SINGLE LEG

Even if you spend months developing counters to the single and double leg takedowns, you're still going to get caught from time to time. A lot of jiu-jitsu practitioners concede to the takedown when an opponent hauls one of their legs off the ground. They figure that they're going down, so there is no use fighting it. I feel this is a bad choice because you're not only allowing your opponent to rack up points on the judges' scorecards, but you are also falling right into his game plan. Resisting the takedown is fairly easy if you learn how to balance on one leg. BJ Penn is a master at this. I have watched him get one of his legs snatched up several times during his UFC bouts, but instead of dropping down to his back, he simply hopped backwards as his opponent wasted energy driving into him. And with both of his opponent's arms tied up with his leg, BJ proceeded to punch away at his opponent's unprotected face. Practicing this drill will not make you immune to takedowns, but it will increase your chances of staying on your feet.

1 My brother and I square off. He has chosen a low jiu-jitsu stance, and I have chosen more of a judo stance.

2 My brother shoots in for a single leg and I am too slow to latch onto his collar to stop him. Immediately I drop left hand to the back of his head and latch onto the back of his collar with my right hand. I use both to push his head down toward his right leg. Although his body is still driving into me, his head is now going in another direction, which takes power away from his shot. To take even more force out of his shot, I lock my arms straight.

3 My brother lifts my knee up to his chest. In order to resist this, I would need to have my feet closer together, but then he could transition to a double leg. Instead, I continue to force his head down toward his right foot, fully extending my arms. Notice how this creates separation between our bodies, which makes it difficult for him to capture my other leg as well. In addition, I place my right foot on the outside of my brother's left leg. I can now push off of his hip with my right shin to further maintain distance between us.

4-5 Determined to get the takedown, my brother continues to drive in. Because he has so much force behind him, I no longer have the ability to keep my arms straight. This is dangerous territory because he is drawing ever closer to my right leg, so I prepare to make my move backwards.

6 Pushing off his head and collar with my hands, as well as pushing off his left leg with my shin, I hop my left foot backwards. Because I am applying so much downward pressure, my foot effortlessly glides across the mat, almost as if I were walking on the moon. I don't want to force the landing of my left foot, because if he is driving in really hard, that could cause me to lose balance and fall backwards. Instead, I let my left foot glide along until it naturally comes down on its own.

7 My brother drives in again, still determined.

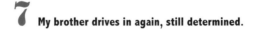

8 Driving down with my arms and pushing off with my right shin, I hop backwards again. This battle could go on and on, but as long as you maintain your composure, your opponent will be burning considerably more energy than you. You can use the time to focus on your options, of which there are many.

SINGLE LEG TO UCHI-MATA

This is another defense for a single leg takedown, except in this situation your opponent has secured your leg really tight between his legs. Generally your defense will be at its highest when your trapped leg is hooked around the outside of your opponent's lead leg. You not only have better balance, but it also allows you to go for triangles and other submissions. When your leg is trapped on the inside things get a little trickier, but this is an excellent technique to employ if you find yourself in such a predicament. Instead of fighting the takedown and trying to stay up on your feet, you're going to control your opponent's far arm, rotate, and then throw him with an uchi-mata. I use this technique all the time in competition, especially when going up against a strict jiu-jitsu practitioner.

1 My brother and I are in a low jiu-jitsu stance, searching for an opening.

2 My brother shoots in, and I miss my chance to latch onto his collar with both hands. Instead, I try to stop his shot by establishing a high grip with my right hand and controlling his right elbow with a sleeve grip.

3 My brother still latches onto my right leg. Because he has gotten so deep, I can't push his head down toward his right foot like I did in the previous technique.

4 My brother brings my left leg up and presses it tightly against his chest, stopping me from putting my right shin on the outside of his left leg. Deciding to use my positioning to transition into an uchi-mata, I arch the toes of my right foot up to ensure that my leg remains between my brother's legs. I still have a right hand high grip on his collar, and I am now using my left sleeve grip to pull his right elbow toward me to weaken his grip on my leg.

5 I hop toward my brother on my left foot and turn my body in a counterclockwise direction at the same time. As I do this, I continue to pull my brother's right elbow toward me, which frees my leg and allows me to arch it back between his legs. Notice that I still have a strong grip on his collar with my right hand, and that I'm using it to rotate my brother's body into the throw.

6 As I continue to rotate my body and pull my brother around with my grips, my right leg hooks my brother's left leg and pulls it off the ground. Notice that my movement is almost like a shoulder roll.

7 I land with my knee dug into my brother's side and my foot on his stomach. Notice that my grips have not changed. I still have the high grip with my right hand and I'm controlling his left elbow with my sleeve grip.

8 Looking to obtain the mount position, I slide my foot across my brother's stomach toward his right side.

9 I slide my right knee down to the mat, keeping it really tight to my brother's right side to hinder him from scrambling away. Here I have obtained the mount position.

10 I lower my body down and hook my feet underneath my brother's legs, securing the mount position. Neither of my grips have changed. I use my high grip to pull my body into my brother and lock everything down.

SINGLE LEG TO SCISSOR THROW

The single leg to scissor throw works great when your opponent has secured a deep single leg and you are in the process of going down. At this point your opponent is so committed and confident that you can usually catch him by surprise with this technique. I have done this move many times in jiu-jitsu competition, and it sets you up for all kinds of foot attacks such as heel hooks.

1 My brother and I are in low jiu-jitsu stances, searching for an opening.

2 My brother shoots in and secures a really deep single leg. I place my left hand on the back of his head to push it down and away, but his left shoulder is too close for me to secure a high grip with my right hand. Instead, I reach my right hand over his back and latch onto his belt.

3 As my brother lifts my leg, trapping it between his legs, he drives into my right thigh with his left shoulder. I have a hard time stopping this without a high grip, so I know that I am going down at this point. I'm already thinking about the scissor throw.

4 As my brother drives his shoulder into my leg and forces me down, I plant my left hand on the mat. Feeling that he has gotten me, my brother drives his head into the takedown. Because I have my grip on his belt, I can tighten everything up and go for the scissor throw.

5 Holding myself up with my right belt grip and my left hand, I wrap my left leg behind my brother's left leg. At the same time, I arch my right foot to trap his right leg, which stops him from stepping backwards to reestablish his balance and base. I am still pushing off with my left hand, and I'm continuing to pull my body close to his with my belt grip. My combined movement locks him in place—he can't stand up or step back. By pushing down with my left leg and pulling my right leg toward me, I cause him to lose balance and start falling backward.

6 Arching back, I finish the throw. The lower half of my body is key here. I'm arching my right foot, maintaining control of my brother's right leg. My left knee is tight against his left leg, locking it in place. My right hand is still tightly gripping his belt in case he wants to try something crafty in his half guard. My left hand is on his heel, which will allow me to go for a toehold, a heel hook, or a straight foot lock.

SINGLE GRIP FOOT SWEEP

Having practiced the standard foot sweep, you now understand exactly when to attack your opponent's foot, which is right as he pushes off for another step or just before his foot plants. Executing foot sweeps with duel grips works best, but some jiu-jitsu opponents will be reluctant to step when you already have your grips, especially if they know that you are proficient in judo. The single grip foot sweep has a high success rate in jiu-jitsu competition because you don't have to engage to get the foot sweep. You simply step, grip with one hand, and then sweep your opponent's foot to launch him into the air. I can't recall how many times I've chucked jiu-jitsu opponents with this technique.

1 My brother and I are in low jiu-jitsu stances, looking for an opening.

2 Deciding that I am going to execute a single grip foot sweep, I take a step forward with my left foot.

3 As I push off with my right foot to reach in for a high grip, my brother gets cautious and leans back. At this point, his primary concern is my right hand. Because my right foot is so far back, he isn't worried about me attacking with it. As a reaction, he latches onto my sleeve as my hand comes forward.

4 Because my brother backed up as I shot my right hand forward, he took weight off his left leg, making it light on the ground. To catch him, I shoot my right foot forward, lifting my big toe and letting my pinky toe scrap along the ground. This allows me to strike his ankle with the bottom of my foot. (It is important to note that this is an explosive move, so you should drive your foot forward with force.) Now that I have swept my brother's foot off the ground, I use my high grip to pull his upper body toward the mat. He has no balance or base to resist because I have just taken out his only stabilizer on his left side.

5 I pull my brother's upper body toward the ground and in a clockwise direction with my right grip. At the same time, I follow through with my sweep. You don't want to strike your opponent's leg and then bring your foot back. You want to sweep his leg up into the air.

6-7 I come down into side control without switching the position of my body. Sometimes the throw can cause a little separation, and you want to close that distance as quickly as possible by pulling yourself down on top of your opponent using your high grip. If you immediately try to switch positions, it can give your opponent a chance to pull guard. Notice that my left hand is up, ready to stop my opponent from pulling me into his guard.

REVERSE: Notice how my right knee is putting pressure on my brother's belt-line, hindering him from pulling guard. If he doesn't make a significant effort to pull me into his guard, I'll grab onto his belt with my left hand to pull my body tight to his. Doing this makes it even harder for him to scramble and trap me between his legs.

UCHI-MATA ON KNEELING OPPONENT

Once you toss an opponent in competition, the other competitors will realize that you're not an everyday jiu-jitsu practitioner. In order to avoid your stand-up skills, many of them will either jump guard or go down to one knee the moment you draw close. If your opponent tries dropping down to one knee, you can still throw him by utilizing this technique. I know that it works in jiu-jitsu competition because my brother executed it flawlessly at a tournament in Santa Cruz against Genki Sudo, who has since become somewhat of a legend in the grappling and MMA world. Genki was ahead on points and dropped to one knee because he thought there was no way my brother could throw

him while he was in that position. A split second later my brother reached down, secured a high grip, and then threw Genki with an uchi-mata. To top it off, my brother quickly transitioned to an armlock and forced Genki to tap by submission. In addition to being an effective technique, it is also a crowd pleaser. Needless to say, my brother was the crowd favorite that day.

1 My brother and I have assumed low jiu-jitsu stances.

2 Pretending to be a jiu-jitsu guy who wants nothing to do with my stand-up, my brother goes down to his right knee as I draw near. The second he does this, I immediately latch onto him with a sleeve and high grip. I use my high grip to pull his body toward me, causing him to lean forward. I use my sleeve grip to pull his right arm toward me, separating his elbow from his body and making it hard for him to ball up. A lot of jiu-jitsu practitioners will doubt that you can throw them from this position, and they'll wait until you draw closer to pull guard.

3 I step my right foot behind my left, but I don't get too close. I don't want my movement to look too aggressive.

4 Still assuming that I can't throw him while he is on one knee, my brother keeps his left knee raised. To capitalize on the situation, I rotate my body in a counterclockwise direction and begin lifting my right leg to hook around the back of his left knee. At the same time, I use my grips to pull my brother's upper body in a counterclockwise direction. To make the most out of the move, I want to pull his body close to me and be explosive in my movement.

5 Continuing to rotate in a counterclockwise direction and pull my brother's upper body with me using my grips, I bend down as I lift my right leg up to capture my brother's left leg.

6 Using the rotation of my body and my right leg, I toss my brother over onto his back. Doing this move from closer range will create more lift, but you can certainly pull it off from the outside. Either way, your opponent will have a very hard time pulling you into his guard once he goes over to his back.

7 While my brother is still in motion from the throw, I drop my right knee into his stomach and assume the standard impact control position.

BACK TO KOSOTO-GARI

A lot of times when your opponent is on all fours and you take his back, he will stand up, making it difficult for you to keep the dominant position. Jiu-jitsu practitioners will try many different things to bring their opponent back down, but few of them work as well as this technique. It works great for jiu-jitsu competition, judo, and MMA. I threw NCAA Champion Josh Koscheck with this move while grappling without a gi.

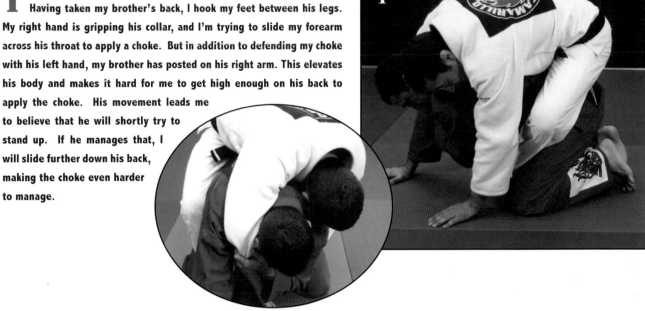

1 Having taken my brother's back, I hook my feet between his legs. My right hand is gripping his collar, and I'm trying to slide my forearm across his throat to apply a choke. But in addition to defending my choke with his left hand, my brother has posted on his right arm. This elevates his body and makes it hard for me to get high enough on his back to apply the choke. His movement leads me to believe that he will shortly try to stand up. If he manages that, I will slide further down his back, making the choke even harder to manage.

2 As my brother plants his left foot, I have no doubt that he is going to stand up to shake me off his back. Because I want to make the most of the back position, I try to peel his defending hand away so I can sink in the choke with my right forearm.

3 My brother manages to stand totally up. Now he has both hands to defend against the choke, and I start to slide down his back.

4 To shake me off his back, my brother reaches his left arm down and peels my left foot out from between his legs. If he is successful in his defense, I will shortly slide down and he will be free to turn and face me.

5 Realizing I have lost the back, I come down on my own. But instead of just dropping down so my brother can face me, I slide my right leg deeper around my brother's left leg. My left foot swings in a counterclockwise direction, causing my chest to face my brother's right side. I keep my grip on his collar tight, which gives me the option of swinging my body back around and reestablishing the back position. Right now I am trying to decide my best option.

6 I have decided that my best option is to go for kosoto-gari. To begin the throw, I release my right grip on my brother's collar and swing my right arm over his head, generating momentum for the throw. At the same time, I rotate my upper body in a counterclockwise direction. It is important to note that my brother will give his best effort to turn into me, so it is important that I generate momentum with my rotation and the swing of my arm.

7 My brother has managed to face me, but now I have turned away from him. It looks like he will take my back, but he can't because of the deep hook I have on his right leg.

8 I use the momentum I generated from my rotation and swinging arm to drop down into a forward roll, making sure to keep my right hook nice and tight around my brother's leg to ensure that he will come with me. In order to be successful with this technique, you need to exaggerate your forward roll movement.

9 I land with my right leg still hooked around my brother's right leg. Right now I am technically in my brother's guard, so I don't want to hang out in this position for long. The moment I land, I'm already starting to move.

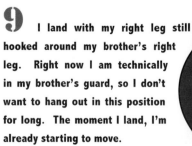

10 I lift my left leg off the ground and start to bring it up and over my brother's right leg to pass his guard.

11 My plant my left foot on my brother's left side. Notice that I have kept my right leg hooked around my brother's right leg to maintain control.

12 I release my right hook on my brother's leg and drop down to the side control position. It is important to note that this entire movement should be done as fast and explosively as possible.

SECTION TWO

FROM THROWS TO SUBMISSIONS

FROM THROWS TO SUBMISSIONS

While on the San Jose State Judo Team, we'd frequently conduct a drill that we called transitions. It entailed squaring off with an opponent, throwing him to the mat, and then trying to finish him in less than twenty seconds with a submission. If you could not finish your opponent in twenty seconds, the match would get stood up and you'd have to start over. With most of my teammates lacking a background in jiu-jitsu, it was hard for many of them to get the finish in the limited amount of time. I never had a problem with this because I trained every afternoon in jiu-jitsu. However, not wanting to take the full twenty seconds to finish my opponent, I started playing around with my style. Instead of waiting until I hit the ground to focus on submissions, I started setting up my submissions the moment I engaged on my feet. I'd get my grips, throw my opponent, and then use my original grips to transition directly into a submission. In just a few weeks, rarely did I need the full twenty seconds to get the finish.

Thrilled with the new addition to my system, I took it one step further and developed what I call the impact control position, which is the most dominant position you can achieve after every throw to limit your opponent's movement. While my teammates were breaking the transitions drill down into two different stages—getting the throw, and then hunting for a submission—I had bridged the gap and made it one fluid motion. I

didn't have to shift gears. I didn't have to re-grip once the fight went down. Every time I stepped forward and put my hands on my opponent, whether it was in judo practice or in jiu-jitsu practice, I was focused on finishing him with a submission. It evolved to the point where I didn't even need to be in control. When I threw an opponent and he escaped my impact control position and went for a reversal, I would often go with the reversal. Because I was still thinking about submissions during the transition, I would catch my opponent before he could get to a dominant position.

If you have practiced all the techniques in this book, then you should have a good understanding of basic judo. The techniques in this section will help you blend judo throws with jiu-jitsu submissions to eliminate wasted time and energy that comes from switching gears. The following techniques will teach you how to better control your opponent once the fight goes to the ground, making the transition from the standing position to the submission even more streamlined. The techniques will also show you how to keep the submission mindset even when you lose control of your opponent after a throw, and this often allows you to catch him off guard. Practicing all the moves in this section will help you combine the different stages of combat into one fluid motion, giving you a leg up on nearly every other competitor out there.

PULLS

As I have mentioned, you do not want to change your grips after you throw because it gives your opponent an opportunity to pull guard or scramble to a dominant position. Instead you want to ride out his thrashing in the standard impact control position using your original grips. This not only requires strong and efficient grips, but also an acquired instinct of keeping your elbows tucked tight against your body. This drill will help you on both fronts. Although it might seem rather silly pulling your body across the mat, the drill should not be overlooked. It can make the difference between controlling your opponent off a throw and transitioning to a submission or losing control of your opponent and having to fight out of his guard. When I trained in Japan at the age of sixteen, we had four practices a day, and we did this drill across and back an Olympic sized mat at the start of every practice. The first day I lost all the skin on my elbows, and everyday after I bled through my gi. It wasn't until I entered my next competition that I realized how much this drill had helped me.

1 This is the starting position of the drill. My hands are balled into fists, elbows tight to my body, legs spread, feet arched with my toes ready to help push my body forward.

2 I straighten my arms with my knuckles facing up. Notice how I have my belt turned to the side to keep the knot from digging into my abdomen.

3 Digging my elbows into the mat and slowly turning my wrists so that my thumbs are pointed up, I pull myself forward. This helps develop the strength needed to keep your elbows in tight to your body, which is extremely important for keeping the standard impact control position. My legs remain relaxed, but to help aid my forward movement, I push off the mat with my toes.

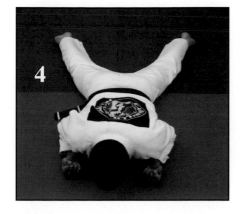

4 This is the end of my pull. My knuckles have turned all the way over and are now facing the mat. This helps develop wrist strength for your grips. My elbows are tight to my body, and my toes are now pointed down because they have helped push me forward. From here, I will arch my feet again and reach forward to execute another pull. You should do this drill across and back the mat at least once every practice.

ARM EXPOSURE

Before transitioning to a submission from the standard impact control position, it is important to first understand when your opponent is vulnerable to attack. If your opponent is lying flat on his back, he can use the mat as a backstop for his arms, which can make it hard to catch him in an armlock. But when he turns onto his side, one of his elbows must lift off the mat, exposing that arm. To be proficient at transitions off of throws, you must not only be able to spot these weaknesses when they arise, but also capitalize on them before they disappear.

1 Lying flat on his back, my brother's defenses are strong. If I hovered over him in the standard impact control position and tried to lift one of his elbows to apply an arm lock, he could simply force his elbow down to the mat to counter.

2 Turning onto his right side, my brother's left arm is exposed and vulnerable because it has lifted off the mat. Now the only backstop he has for his arm is his body. If I were on top of him, I would have a much better chance of securing an armlock. He would most likely try to defend by rolling down to his back.

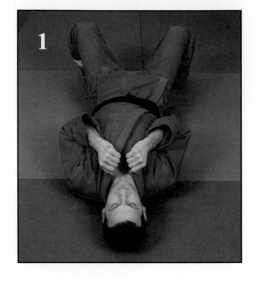

3 My brother has rolled flat onto his back where his defenses are strong.

4 My brother rolls onto his left side, exposing his right arm. If I were on top of him, I would now try to attack his vulnerable arm. To defend, he would again roll onto his back. If you have strong grips and a good knowledge of when your opponent is at his weakest, you can go back and forth until you catch him.

QUICK ARMLOCK SWITCH

Now that you understand when your downed opponent's arm is most vulnerable, it is time to learn how to capitalize on his vulnerability. In this drill, you have just thrown your opponent and achieved the mount position. As your opponent tries to turn his body to escape, you are going to rotate your body so you can attack his exposed arm. Although most of the time your opponent's movements will be explosive, forcing you to react with speed of your own, this drill should be done slow at first. As you get the hang of it, increase your speed in increments until you're going live. Practicing this drill will help you understand when your opponent's defenses are at their weakest. It will also increase your reaction speed.

1 I'm in the mount position. Because my brother is lying flat on his back, he can force his elbows to the mat and use it as a backstop if I attack one of his arms. Here his defense is at its highest.

2 Trying to escape, my brother quickly turns onto his left side. As his right arm comes up, I rotate my body in a clockwise direction and come up onto my left foot. I also trap his arm with my left hand. Notice how I dig my left leg into his side, which helps keep his right shoulder elevated. My right hand is poised to trap is leg if need be. Here my brother's defenses are weak.

3 To avoid getting his right arm caught in an armlock, my brother quickly rolls to his right side. I secure the standard mount as he rolls, but I'm ready to rotate in a counterclockwise direction and come up on my right foot. Notice how my right hand is already preparing to trap my brother's left arm.

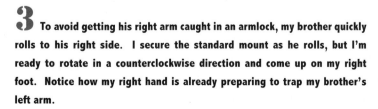

4 As my brother rolls up onto his right side, I trap his arm with my right hand, rotate my body in a counterclockwise direction, and come up onto my left foot. Now I am back in the side mount position.

5 I anticipate that my brother will roll back to his left side, so I have already brought my right knee up to make the most of his arm exposure.

6 As my brother rolls onto his left side, I trap his arm with my left hand and transition to the side mount. I've had enough of this back and forth game, so I'm ready to throw my right leg over his head to finish the armlock.

7 One step ahead of my brother this time, I switch my hands so that I am now trapping his right arm with my right hand. I plant my left hand on the side of his head and push down so I can throw my leg over.

8 Having moved my left foot to the left side of my brother's head, I wrap my left arm around my brother's right arm. Notice that the crook of my arm has fallen against the crook in my brother's arm. My right hand is above my brother's forearm.

9 I fall back, keeping my brother's body and head pinned to the mat with my legs. As I do this, the crook of my left arm slides up his right arm. Notice how his right wrist comes down onto my right wrist. It is almost like I am doing a triangle choke on his arm. By doing it this way, it ensures that my brother can't wriggle his arm free. It is the most efficient way to execute an armlock.

10 Still pinning my brother's body and head to the ground with my legs, I arch my hips upwards. I haven't changed the position of my hands. With my brother's elbow hyperextended, he taps in submission. You can certainly do this move by latching onto your opponent's wrist with your hands, but this way is much more efficient. It leaves your opponent with no wiggle room.

QUICK ARMLOCK SWITCH #2

After throwing your opponent and securing the standard impact control position, there is a good chance that he will turn into you in an attempt to get to his knees. This is especially true if your opponent is a strict jiu-jitsu practitioner. Although this will make it difficult to attack the arm closest to you, it will expose your opponent's far arm. Drilling this technique over and over will make you quick at transitioning to the far arm and increase your chance of getting a submission immediately after the throw. As in the previous drill, you want to start at about twenty percent speed and slowly progress toward a live roll.

1 I have just thrown my brother and landed in the standard impact control position. Immediately he starts to roll into me in an attempt to pull me into his guard. I still have the same sleeve and collar grip I established before the throw.

2 I release my right grip on my brother's collar and hook my right hand behind his left elbow to control it.

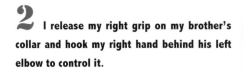

3 Releasing my left sleeve grip and posting my hand on the mat, I throw my left leg over my brother's head. Notice how I am applying pressure with my leg to the left side of his head, cranking his neck to the right. My right hand is still controlling his left elbow.

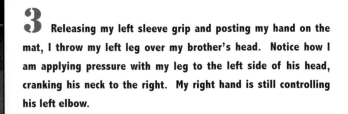

4 I swing my left knee around to my brother's left side and then sit down. Basically, I have spun my body in a counterclockwise direction around his left arm. Although you can't see it in this photo, my left shin is digging into my brother's side and my knee is pointed toward the ceiling.

5 My brother begins turning into me. Realizing that it will be hard to lock in the submission, I decide to abandon it. To deal with his defense, I wrap the crook of my left arm over his trapped arm so I can post my right hand on the mat.

6 Keeping my brother's arm trapped with my left arm, I post my right hand on the mat so I have leverage to turn and stand up.

7 As my brother continues to turn into me, I use my posted right hand to lift my right leg and plant my right foot on the mat. Notice that I am about to lose the trap on my brother's left arm, but because he is turning into me, I am going to trap his far arm.

8 Posting my right foot behind me, I hook my left arm underneath my brother's right arm as he turns into me.

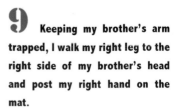

9 Keeping my brother's arm trapped, I walk my right leg to the right side of my brother's head and post my right hand on the mat.

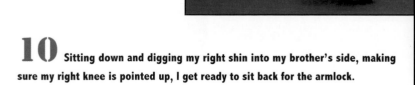

10 Sitting down and digging my right shin into my brother's side, making sure my right knee is pointed up, I get ready to sit back for the armlock.

11 To defend, my brother turns into me again. I realize it will be hard to lock in the submission, so I abandon it. I wrap the crook of my right arm over his right arm so I can post my left hand back, giving me the leverage to get up and change position.

12 As my brother turns into me, I dig my right arm underneath his left arm to trap it.

13 Still trapping my brother's left arm, I come up onto my feet.

14 Keeping my right hand locked behind my brother's left elbow, I push his head to the mat with my left hand so I can walk my left foot around to the other side.

15 I bring my left foot around to the left side of my brother's head.

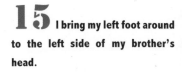

16 Sitting down after I finish my counterclockwise rotation, I dig my left shin into my brother's side, making sure that my left knee is pointed up. From here I can sit back for the submission or continue with the drill.

CUTTING CORNERS FOR ARMLOCKS

Maintaining a dominant position after throwing your opponent is not easy. You just scored big points on the judges' scorecards by taking your opponent down, and he will most likely move hard and fast to pull you into his guard. If you've retained the grips that you established while in the standing position, then you'll usually be in good shape. But you'll still only have a split second to figure out your submission possibilities and then go for one. And when you go for your submission, your opponent will most certainly scramble and put up a fight. The chances are he will throw up a blockade or partially defend your submission attempt. If you do not alter your submission to deal with the blockade or defense, the chances are you will miss the submission. That is why it is so important to learn how to cut corners. It will give you options when things don't go exactly as planned, which is most of the time. When you learn how to maximize your efficiency with little movement, the end result is usually a finish.

1 Mounted on my brother, I am going for the standard armlock. I have secured his left arm with my left arm, and now all I have to do is throw my right leg over his head, fall back, and then arch my hips. But something isn't going right. My brother has grabbed onto my left leg with his right hand, and he's trying to rip it away to steal my leverage. If he manages this, I won't be able to extend his arm with any real force, and I will have lost the submission. To deal with the development, I am trying to peel his hand away with my right hand.

2 I don't feel comfortable throwing my right leg over to the right side of my brother's head. If I do that and then drop back for the armlock, he will use his right hand to peel my right leg off of his head, and then I won't have any leverage to finish. To deal with the new development, I stick my right foot underneath his head. Notice that my right toes are connecting with my left heel underneath his head. This gives me the leverage to finish the armlock. I have just cut a major corner in an attempt to salvage the submission.

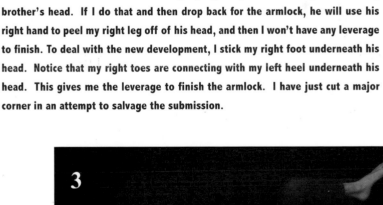

3 Squeezing my knees together, my brother is locked so tight he can't rip my leg away or escape. I now have the leverage to fall back and finish the armlock.

COUNTERING ARMLOCK DEFENSE

This is another example of cutting corners to find a fast solution to a problem. When you throw your leg over your opponent's head to finish an armlock, he will have a natural reaction, especially if he trains judo or jiu-jitsu. Most of the time he will use one of his hands to shove your leg off of his head. This not only takes away your leverage to finish the submission, but it also gives your opponent an avenue to escape. In most jiu-jitsu competitions you see this counter executed half a dozen times, and usually the competitor trying to apply the armlock will abandon the submission. This doesn't have to be the case if you train to cut corners. Most of the time there is an answer to your opponent's defense that allows you to finish the submission. In situations where your opponent stops an armlock by pushing your leg off his head, the answer is simple and straightforward.

1 I am in the standard armlock position, trying to throw my right leg over my brother's head to get leverage to drop back and finish. My brother's natural reaction is to push my leg off his head with his right hand. If he can manage this, he is certain that he can escape.

2 My brother has almost completed his defense. He has peeled my right leg off his head with his right hand, and now he is trying to trap my leg underneath his head. If I try to drop back now to finish, I won't have the leverage needed to hyperextend his arm.

3 While my brother is still trying to trap my right leg behind his head, I lift my left leg and move my foot toward the left side of his head.

4 I hook my left foot underneath my brother's head. Locking my left leg tight gives me the leverage to drop back and finish the submission. If I hadn't cut a major corner, the chances are I would have lost the submission.

COUNTERING ARMLOCK DEFENSE #2

When going for a submission, you should always expect your opponent to counter. This is especially true with armlocks. They are so common that even white belts know the counters. If you head into an armlock simply hoping for the best, there is a good chance that you will miss the submission and land yourself in a compromising position. However, there is a large chance that you will end the fight if you head into the submission armed with an answer to your opponent's likely counters. It is another example of how cutting corners can win a match.

1 I have my brother in a triangle position and I'm dropping back to extend his arm. In defense, my brother is peeling my left leg off of his head so he can scoot his hips out. Even if I were to drop all the way back and arch my hips, I wouldn't have enough leverage to finish.

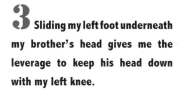

2 Having successfully peeled my left leg off of his head, my brother is confident that he can sit up, pass my guard, and move into the side control position. To begin countering his defense, I turn over to my left hip so I can drive my left knee down into his chest and keep him on the mat.

3 Sliding my left foot underneath my brother's head gives me the leverage to keep his head down with my left knee.

4 Keeping his head down with my left knee, I throw my right leg across my brother's face, giving me the leverage to arch my hips and finish the armlock.

ELBOW CONTROL

Submissions should not be set up after the fight has hit the ground; they should be set up the moment you grip your opponent in the standing position. This is possible by using your grips to gain control of your opponent's elbows. If you already have elbow control when the fight goes down, then you can instantly obtain the positioning needed to finish your opponent with a submission. Waiting to achieve elbow control only gives your opponent an opportunity to scramble or launch at attack of his own. If you are training without a gi or getting ready for MMA competition, you should cup the back of your opponent's arm to gain control of his elbow. Developing strong elbow control skills in the standing position will improve your ground game significantly.

1 Here I have applied a standard sleeve grip to tighten the gi around my brother's arm and gain control of his elbow. Notice that my hand is slightly above his elbow. If he pulls his arm away, I use my hand as a backstop to limit his motion. It will make transitions much more efficient. It will also set you up for flying attacks, which you will learn about in the next section. Just as with the sleeve grip I previously applied lower on my brother's arm, I have the seam in my palm for the strongest grip.

2 I tighten everything up by pulling his arm closer to my body. Notice that my elbow is tight against my body to ensure that I'm strong on my left side.

IMPACT CONTROL

Now that you know how to establish your grips and chuck an opponent, it's time to spend a little more time developing proper positioning when you land. As you learned in the previous section, different throws require different grips. Some require a pistol grip, others require a high grip, and still others require a really deep belt grip. The various throws will also land you in different positions on the ground. Below are the impact control positions for the throws you have already learned, as well as a few impact control positions you can employ when things go wrong. It is important to familiarize yourself with the basics by getting into these positions on a training partner and having him try to escape. Once you understand the fundamentals, such as how to use your original grips to maintain control of your opponent, transitioning into a submission will become a whole lot easier.

1 This is the standard impact control position for a variety of throws that rely upon the pistol grip, such as harai-goshi, uchi-mata, and tai-otoshi. We have just landed, so I want to keep everything tight to gain control. My left hand sleeve grip is already controlling my brother's right arm just above his elbow, and I want to pull up on his arm with my left shoulder to keep his shoulder off the ground. As we learned with arm exposure, the moment he drops his shoulders to the mat, his ability to defend is greater. Right here he could bend his arm down to his head and I would still be able to apply upward pressure on his elbow. With my right pistol grip, I drive down to keep my brother pinned to the floor. At the same time, I also pull my right arm and his collar toward my left arm. This keeps everything extremely tight and makes it very hard for my brother to roll. If he turns away from me, he will expose his right arm and I will instantly transition into an armlock or slide my right knee across his belly and obtain the mount position. By keeping my original grips and using proper technique, I have maintained control and made my brother vulnerable to submissions.

2 This is the standard impact control position for a variety of throws done with a high grip. These throws can include a high grip harai-goshi, a high grip tai-otoshi, and a high grip uchi-mata when your opponent is on one knee. You will gain control over your opponent just as you did in the previous impact control position.

3 Sometimes when you land after throwing your opponent, you lose one of your grips. That is what happened here. Instead of trying to reestablish my pistol grip or high grip with my right hand, I latch onto my brother's belt because it is easier to get a firm hold on. Once I have my grip, I pull up on his belt, which in turn drives my right knee deeper into his stomach. This puts more pressure on your opponent than any other impact control position. Notice that my left grip has remained the same—I'm pulling up on his right elbow, keeping his shoulder off the ground and exposing his arm.

4 You can use a really deep grip on your opponent's belt to throw him with tai-otoshi, uchi-mata, harai-goshi, and osoto-gari, and this is how you should land. I have my right knee on my brother's stomach and I'm keeping his right shoulder off the ground by pulling his elbow up with my left sleeve grip. My right grip is different than the previous technique because my hand is still trapped somewhat behind his back. I pull up on his belt with my hand, but because my wrist is bent, I increase my gripping strength by driving my right elbow down and placing it against my right knee. This locks everything tight and makes it very hard for my brother to move. It can take some time to perfect this technique, which is why you should practice it with a training partner as much as possible.

5 There are all kinds of throws you can do with an under-hook, such as tai-otoshi and osoto-gari, and it is important to know how to land properly. In this particular situation, I used an under-hook to force my brother from his low jiu-jitsu stance to a high stance so I could throw him. My right hand is still hooked underneath my brother's left arm, and I have my grip on his collar. It is important that you don't land with head and arm control because that would give your opponent access to your back. I am using my left sleeve grip above his elbow to pull his arm in close to my body. My feet are spread apart, giving me the ability to move quickly if needed. From here, I can attack either his far arm or his near arm by employing the techniques previously shown.

IMPACT CONTROL VARIABLE #1

After throwing your opponent with osoto-gari, harai-goshi, uchi-mata, or tai-otoshi, the armlock is one of the easiest submissions to transition into from the standard impact control position. There are many ways to handle the transition, but the one described below is by far the most efficient.

1 The moment I land after the throw, I assume the standard impact control position. From here I am going to transition right to the armlock.

2 Going for the armlock, I collapse my right elbow so that it is pressing against my right leg. This will stop my brother from sneaking his right leg up between my body and right arm and pulling me into his guard. At the same time, I arch my right foot and dig it into his right armpit. This sets me up for trapping his right arm.

3 I am in the middle of sweeping my left leg around to the left side of my brother's head. As I do this, I release my left grip on his sleeve and let the crook of my left arm slide up to his wrist. This is how I do most of my armlocks because it provides better control of my opponent's wrist if he tries to rotate his arm free. To keep his arm straight, I arch my hips forward into his elbow. Notice that my right arm is still locked to my right leg, keeping my brother from lifting his right leg and pulling me into his guard. It is hard for my brother to sit up here because I am jamming my hips forward, closing any distance he tries to create.

4 I have swept my left leg around to the left side of my brother's head. It is important to notice the arch in my right foot, and how I have planted my foot deep into my brother's armpit. I'm keeping his right arm straight with my hips, and I'm just about to drop back and apply more pressure.

5 As I drop back, I dig my right elbow into my body and use my right grip on my brother's collar to pull him up on top of me. This will keep his body snug against me. Space is your enemy with this submission. At the same time, I am applying downward pressure on his head with my left leg. I still have his right arm trapped in the crook of my left arm. My right shin is dug into his right side, and my right foot is still buried deep in his armpit.

6 I have pulled my brother's body so far on top of me that his left arm is actually exposed. Notice how the toes of my right foot are visible just beneath my left foot. With my right shin still digging into his side, I apply downward pressure on his right wrist with my left arm and arch my hips.

7 My brother is stubborn and refuses to tap, so I let my right grip on his collar go and double up on his left arm. As I apply downward pressure with my arms and arch my hips, my brother quickly taps.

IMPACT CONTROL VARIABLE #2

The previous technique described how to transition to an armlock from the standard impact control position when you have a sleeve and collar grip. This technique describes how to transition to an armlock from impact control when you have a sleeve and high grip, which is usually a result of throwing your opponent with harai-goshi, uchi-mata, osoto-gari, or tai-otoshi. It is the same submission, except now you will be pulling higher up on your opponent's collar. It doesn't matter how comfortable you were with the previous technique; you don't want to establish different grips after you throw. You want to use the ones you already have.

1 I have just thrown my brother with uchi-mata using a high grip. I assume the impact control position by planting my right knee into his stomach, lifting his right shoulder off the ground using my sleeve grip, and pinning him to the mat with my high collar grip.

2 As I did in the previous technique, I dig my lower right shin into my brother's armpit, arch my foot, and wrap my toes around his right shoulder. I continue to drive his right side to the ground using my high grip, as well as continue to lift his right shoulder with my sleeve grip.

3 I am in the process of sweeping my left leg around to the left side of my brother's head. I have let go of my grip on his sleeve and allowed the crook of my arm to slide up to his wrist. Notice that I still have my grip on his collar, and I'm still punching down. It is also important to notice my right knee. I have slid it deep across his chest to block him from lifting his right leg. If I didn't block his leg and he got his knee on the inside, he could potentially catch me in an armlock by throwing his left leg over my head.

4 My left foot has come all the way around to the left side of my brother's head. Notice how I am really tight against my brother, stopping him from wedging his right knee to the inside and setting up an armlock of his own. You have to be really conscious of closing any distance your opponent tries to create.

5 I roll onto my back, pulling my brother into me using my high grip on his collar. His right wrist is still trapped in the crook of my left arm.

6 Letting my right grip on his collar go, I double up on his arm and pull it down to my chest. At the same time, I arch my hips upward. As you can see, my brother is tapping in submission.

IMPACT CONTROL VARIABLE #3

When you secure the impact control position, your opponent will usually turn into you or turn away from you. Judo players will usually turn away from you in an attempt to get to all fours and avoid a pin. Jiu-jitsu practitioners work well from on their back, and they will usually turn into you to protect their exposed arm and pull you into their guard. This technique works great for the guy who turns into you. Once you put some time into practicing this technique, you should be able to land it a high percentage of the time.

1 I have secured the standard impact control position with a sleeve and collar grip.

2 Worried about his exposed arm, my brother immediately turns into me. Instead of fighting him, I let him come because it exposes his opposite arm. As he reaches with his left arm, he creates space between his left elbow and his body. I throw my right hand into the gap, trapping his arm. At the same time, I plant my left hand on his head and push down. This makes it very difficult for him to move, which will make it much harder for him to trap my left leg as I swing it around to the left side of his head.

3 I swing my left leg around to my brother's left side and plant my foot. Notice that I have continued to apply downward pressure to my brother's head. I also wrap my right hand around my brother's arm just above the elbow. To keep him from trying to wriggle his arm free, I drive my right shoulder down and eliminate space between us.

4 Now that I have gotten my left foot around his head, I plant my left hand on the mat. Starting to turn my body in a clockwise direction, I bend my right knee so that it will trap my brother's head when I sit down. I am still controlling his right arm with my grip on his sleeve.

5 I finish rotating in a clockwise direction and sit down. My right leg is now locked over my brother's head, and I am pinching my knees together. Realizing what has just happened, my brother begins to thrash in an attempt to escape.

6 With my right hand still controlling above my brother's elbow, stopping him from moving his arm from side to side, I throw the crook of my left arm over the top of his wrist to keep his arm from rotating. You can also do this armlock by simply latching onto your opponent's wrist with your hands, but then you run the risk of your opponent wiggling his arm free or overpowering you with sheer strength. The way I teach allows much less wriggle room for your opponent, and I think that you will find that you land your armlocks a larger percentage of the time when using it.

7 As I fall back, I let the crook of my left arm slide up to my brother's wrist. I throw my right hand over the top for added control.

IMPACT CONTROL VARIABLE #4

This is a great submission to transition into when your opponent drops from the standing position down to one knee and you throw him with uchi-mata. At the same time that you spin around, you lock in a baseball choke.

1 From the standing position, my brother dropped down to one knee and I threw him with uchi-mata. As we landed, I lost my grip on his right sleeve, which happens often. Instead of trying to reestablish that grip, I get a high grip on his right collar. I still have the high grip I established just prior to the throw, and I am driving my right knee down into his upper chest.

2 I keep my right knee across my brother's chest, but I place my foot on the outside, hooking my foot around his side. Even if he kicks his legs up, he will not be able to trap or hook my leg and capture me in his guard.

3 Keeping my right knee on my brother's chest, I kick my left leg over his body and plant my foot on the mat. Notice that I still have my grips on either side of his head.

4 Now that my left leg is safely over my brother's body, I drop my right knee to the mat and plant my left knee into his stomach. To do this, I have turned my body slightly in a clockwise direction. I still have both grips on his collar.

5 Driving my left knee into my brother's stomach, I post my right foot on the mat to my right. Notice that as I rotate, my left wrist and forearm are working their way across my brother's throat.

6 I step my right foot in a counterclockwise direction and follow up with my left knee. Because I have kept my elbows tight to my body, my rotation has driven my left wrist into my brother's throat. The more I rotate, the deeper my wrist sinks. When done correctly, the positioning of your hands should look like you're holding a baseball bat. As you can see, my brother is already tapping.

IMPACT CONTROL VARIABLE #5

This is an option for an armlock when you use an under-hook to throw your opponent with tai-otoshi, osoto-gari, harai-goshi, or uchi-mata. It is important to maintain the under-hook when you land. If you don't, your opponent will have access to your back. From here you can attack your opponent's far arm as you did in the previous move, but for this technique we're focusing on the near arm, which is already within your control.

1 As we land, my brother attempts to hook his left arm over the top of my right so he can roll me over the top of him and to his left.

2 Before my brother can secure my right arm, I pop up and double my grips up on his right elbow. Although I have planted my right knee on his stomach, I am not applying much pressure. By staying up on the toes of my right foot, I am allowing him to roll to his left, which will help set up the armlock.

3 Using both of my grips and my body weight, I push my brother's right elbow across his body. At the same time, I dig my knee deep into his abdomen. Notice how his right shoulder is elevated off the mat, exposing his arm.

4 Still controlling my brother's elbow with my right grip, I wrap the crook of my left arm around his right arm. At the same time, I begin to sweep my left leg around to the left side of my brother's head. My brother realizes what is going on and tries to drop his right elbow, but he can't because I have my body and weight pressed tightly against his right arm, keeping it straight. Notice how my head is back toward his legs, which makes it easier for me to sweep my left leg around to the left side of his head. If my head were pointed straight up, this would be harder and take longer to achieve.

5 My left foot has come around to the left side of my brother's head. It is important that you make this transition quickly to limit your opponent's opportunity to escape. The crook of my left arm is wrapped tightly around my brother's right wrist.

6 As I drop back, I squeeze my knees together. Notice that I still have my right grip on my brother's elbow. I'm using that grip to pull his elbow toward me as I arch my hips upward and pull down on his arm with the crook of my left arm. Also notice how I have dropped back toward his legs. If I had dropped back straight out to his side, he would have a greater opportunity to escape.

OVERTHROWN ARMLOCK

A lot of times you have to exaggerate a throw to guarantee its success. As a result, your opponent will often try to use his momentum to roll you in the direction of the throw as he lands. This happened when I was grappling with Crosley Gracie. I threw him with a powerful osoto-gari. He had so much forward momentum when he landed that he tried rolling me in the direction I had just thrown him. After executing such a beautiful throw, I decided I wasn't going to let that happen and posted my elbow to stop my momentum. Well, my elbow planted but my body kept going. A few weeks later I was on a table getting my shoulder operated on. Instead of posting my elbow, I should have allowed him to roll me and focused on attacking his arm while in the middle of the roll. The technique described below would have worked perfectly if done correctly. It's perfect because when an opponent rolls you after a throw, he usually straightens his arm, which allows you to apply this technique. You will be surprised at how often it works. Your opponent will be so focused on tossing you over that rarely will he see the submission coming until it's too late. At the Canadian Open, I beat one of the top Canadian Judoka with this move in the third round.

1 Because I have exaggerated my throw to guarantee its success, I land with my head on my brother's left side in the impact control position. My waist is over his waist, and he uses my positioning and his momentum to roll me in the direction of the throw. Notice how even though I am out of position, I use my grip on his left sleeve to pull up on his elbow and keep his arm straight. This doesn't worry my brother because he is in the process of rolling me and doesn't think there is anyway I can attack his arm. I still have my collar grip with my right hand, and I keep my right elbow locked close to my body. I don't want him to be able to separate my elbow from my side.

2 I know that my brother is going to roll me over, so I concede. I keep everything tight, preparing to attack.

3 As my brother rolls me down onto my shoulder, I slip my right knee between our bodies, planting it on his chest. This will create separation between us for my attack. Notice that neither of my grips have changed.

4 As my brother achieves his goal of rolling me over, I throw my left leg over his head and hook underneath it. At the same time, I release my left grip on his sleeve and wrap the crook of my left arm around his right arm. Although you can't see it here, I still have my right grip on his collar.

5 By keeping my right grip on my brother's collar, it makes it very hard for him to pull his right arm out of my grasp and escape by coming up to his knees. I am also keeping my right shin tight to his body, further limiting his mobility. To lock in the submission, I pull his right arm to my chest with the crook of my left arm and arch my hips toward the mat.

KOUCHI-GARI TRANSITION

Although you can apply the armlocks described earlier in this section after throwing your opponent with kouchi-gari, this technique is the quickest and most efficient from your landing position off the throw.

1 This is the position I have landed in after throwing my brother with kouchi-gari. My right leg is straddled over the top of my brother's right leg, pinning it to the mat. I'm driving down on his collar with my right grip to keep his upper body pinned, and I'm pulling his right arm up with my sleeve grip, exposing his arm. If my brother were to throw his left leg up and over my head, I would drop my upper body slightly down and lock my arms, creating a solid shield to stop him from breaking through and pulling me into his guard.

2 I collapse my right elbow down into his stomach. Notice that I still have a pistol grip with my right hand, which allows me to drop my elbow without bending my wrist. I also drop my hip down, making it harder for him to pull me into his guard with his left leg. I continue to lift his right elbow with my sleeve grip.

3 I slide my right shin up into my brother's armpit. My right elbow is still dug into his abdomen, and I'm still pulling up on his right arm with my sleeve grip. I am also driving off with my left foot to keep my brother's right shoulder elevated and his arm exposed.

4 Still with a tight grip on my brother's collar, I drop my bottom to the mat and bring my left knee in to trap his arm between my legs. I let go of my grip on his sleeve and slide the crook of my left arm up to his wrist by driving my shoulders back. Notice here how I am controlling both sides of my brother's body.

5 Throwing my left leg over my brother's head, I let go of my collar grip and double up on his arm. To lock in the submission, I use my arms to pull his right wrist to my chest and arch my hips upward.

KOUCHI-GARI SPINNING ARMLOCK

Sometimes you don't land perfectly when you throw an opponent, making it hard to immediately assume the standard impact control position. In the photos below I give an example of such a landing. As you can see, I was unable to control my brother's left side with my collar grip, giving him the ability to scoot his hips out, lift his left side, and work around my body in an attempt to pull me into his half guard. However, my brother is still not totally at ease. Because I have maintained my original grips, I still have control of his elbow. My brother knows he is weak on that side of his body, and he is worried that I will attack the arm I control. He doesn't expect me to attack his far arm, but that is exactly what I'm going to do. Utilizing this technique allows you to transition from an awkward position into a submission.

1 After throwing my brother, my body lands farther away from his right side than I like. Notice that my I don't have the leverage I normally do with my right collar grip, making it hard to keep his left shoulder pinned to the mat. I also don't have my knee on his stomach. Anticipating that he will try to bring his left side up to pull me into his half guard, I keep my left knee up and plant my foot on the mat.

2 My brother does exactly what I thought he'd do. He starts hipping out and reaching his left hand around to control my right leg. Currently he is worried about me attacking his right arm because it is exposed. This takes his focus away from his left arm, which he has just exposed by reaching for my leg.

3 As my brother wraps his left arm around my leg, I push off with my left foot, rotating on my right foot in a counterclockwise direction. Notice that I still have my grip on his right sleeve. If I let that go, he can come up to his knees and be safe from my submission attempt. Right now I am simply creating an angle to attack his exposed left arm.

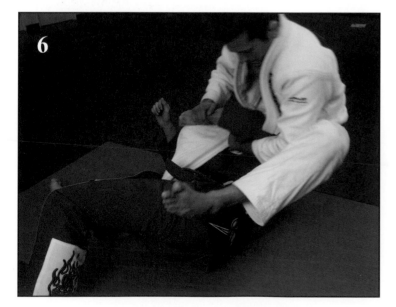

4 As I continue to rotate on my right foot in a counterclockwise direction, notice how my brother's left arm becomes exposed. I am still latched onto his right arm with my sleeve grip, which causes my brother to focus on regaining control of his right arm.

5 As my left foot plants on my brother's left side, I let go of his right sleeve and immediately trap his left wrist with my right hand. At the same time, I also reach my left hand underneath his elbow for further control. Notice how my right foot is between his legs. Here he is not trapping my leg, but this technique would work just as well if he had it wrapped up in his half guard.

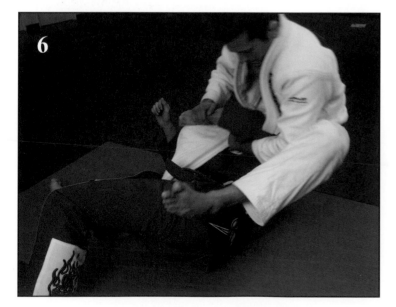

6 Still driving my left hand beneath my brother's left elbow, I throw my left foot up on top of his hip.

7 Having reached my left hand underneath my brother's left elbow, I latch onto my right wrist with my left hand. With my left foot on top of his hip, I drop to the mat on my left side.

8 I rotate my body so that my back is flat on the mat. As I do this, my left leg comes over my brother's body and pins him to the mat. I am still holding his left wrist with my right hand, and my left arm is dug underneath his elbow.

9 As I sit back, the crook of my left arm slides up my brother's left arm, straightening it out.

10 Arching my hips and pinning my brother's arm to my chest, I finish the submission. Notice how I almost have a chokehold on my brother's wrist. This is the most efficient way to finish this armlock.

HALF-GUARD ARMLOCK

As I just mentioned, sometimes it is difficult to land in the standard impact control position after throwing your opponent. When you land funny and your opponent is quick to react, you will often find yourself trapped in his half guard. If that happens to be the case, this technique can come in quite handy.

1 My throw doesn't go quite right, and I land in an awkward position. Quick to react, my brother traps my left leg between his legs, putting me in his half guard. I have control of his head with a right high grip, and I'm already reaching my left hand into the small gap between his right arm and side.

2 Having slipped my left arm underneath my brother's right arm, I release my right high grip and lock my hands together. I use my new grips to tighten my body against my brother's body.

3 With my left leg still trapped between my brother's legs, I rotate my body in a counterclockwise direction and bring my left knee up toward his head. As I do this, I slip my right elbow over the top of his head. His head is now pinched between my right knee and right elbow.

4 I plant my right hand on the back of my brother's head and push it down and away. Because I still have my left arm hooked underneath his right arm, this motion pulls his right arm away from his body, making it vulnerable to attack.

5 Because I was pushing down on my brother's head with my right hand, I can easily bring my right leg over and hook it around the right side of his head. Notice how you can see the knuckles of my left hand. I am using that hand to cup just above my brother's right elbow. It is very hard for him to escape from this position. My left leg is still trapped between his legs.

6 Posting on my right hand and left foot, I walk my body around in a counterclockwise direction. As I do this, I use my left grip on my brother's right elbow to lift his shoulder and further expose his arm.

7 Having walked my body in a counterclockwise direction, I post harder on my right arm and left foot to lift my right knee so I can slide my foot across the mat underneath me. I'm still controlling my brother's elbow with my left grip, pulling his arm over his chest as I continue my rotation.

8 Completing my rotation, I use my posted right hand to sit down. Then I lift my right foot and place it on my brother's abdomen, trapping his arm between my legs.

9 Continuing to slide my right foot across my brother's abdomen, I hook it around the outside of my brother's left knee. At the same time, I hook my left foot around the inside of his left knee. Turning my feet together and locking on his leg, I have just gained some serious leverage. Although I am still trapped in my brother's half guard, it is very hard for him to move in this position.

10 I release my left grip on my brother's elbow and slide the crook of my left arm up to his wrist. As in previous moves we have done, I place my right hand behind my brother's arm, assuming a choke position to maintain the best control over his arm.

11 Dropping back, I finish the submission by squeezing my legs straight, which puts pressure on my thighs and gives me leverage to straighten my brother's arm. It is a very technical move, but also very efficient.

FOOT SWEEP TO ARMLOCK

When you execute a foot sweep it can be difficult to land in the standard impact control position. Trying to reposition your body to acquire the impact control position will take time and space, giving your opponent an opportunity to escape. To keep that from happening, it is often better to transition to a submission from your natural landing position.

1 I just foot swept my brother and this is how I landed. My right foot is creeping up toward his belt-line, and I have lost my grip on his sleeve.

2 My brother drops his left elbow toward the ground to keep me from attacking it. As he does this, I reach my left hand between my legs and latch onto his left sleeve just above his elbow. Notice that I am keeping my left elbow tight against my body.

3 I slide my right leg off my brother's body, and I wedge the lower portion of my leg beneath his arm. As I do this, I establish a grip on his left pants leg with my right hand to keep his knee pinned to the mat.

4 Posting my right fist on the mat to stop my brother from moving his left leg and pulling me into his guard, I walk my body around in a counterclockwise direction. Notice that I still have my grip on my brother's sleeve with my left hand.

5 Completing my rotation, I plant my left foot on the right side of my brother's head. As do this, I continue to use my left shoulder to pull his left arm and shoulder off the mat. Notice how my right leg is blocking my brother from dropping his left elbow to the mat.

6 I let my grip on my brother's pants leg go and wrap the crook of my right arm around his left wrist. Pinching my knees together to trap his arm, I drop down to my back.

7 I throw my right foot over the top of my left foot to bar my brother's head, and then I drop all the way back to lock in the armbar.

LOW FIREMAN'S CARRY TO ARMLOCK

There are a lot of good wrestlers and judo players out there who have mastered the low fireman's carry. After securing just a single grip on your gi, they shoot in for one of your legs and then hoist you off the ground. A good friend of mine has got this moved pegged, and he catches me in it all the time. But instead of conceding to the throw and taking the impact, I use my time in the air to transition into a submission. Although my friend's intent was to humiliate me with a throw, he ends up tapping in submission the moment we hit the mat. If you are quick with this technique, your opponent will never see the submission coming.

1 My brother and I are squared off, searching for an opening.

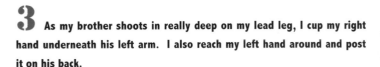

2 My brother latches onto my right sleeve with his left hand. Because he is keeping his distance, I expect that he might try to throw me with a low fireman's carry. I'm already thinking about countering with a submission if he goes for the throw.

3 As my brother shoots in really deep on my lead leg, I cup my right hand underneath his left arm. I also reach my left hand around and post it on his back.

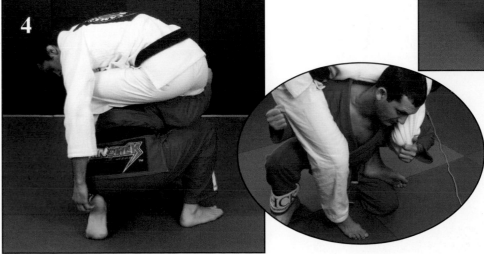

4 Rotating my body in a clockwise direction, I step my left foot around and place it on the inside of my brother's left knee. I reach my left hand down toward his left hamstring muscle. My combined movements are redirecting his throw.

5 As my brother starts his throw, I cup my left hand around his left hamstring muscle.

6 As my brother heads further into his throw, I execute a forward shoulder roll. It is important to notice that in my rotation I have slipped my left leg to the inside of my brother's body. I have also started to trap his right arm with my right leg. As I continue with my shoulder roll, I am going to use my legs to force my brother to come with me in the roll. Here I have already destroyed my brother's throw.

7 Continuing into my shoulder roll, my right leg hooks my brother's right arm and my left leg hooks across his body to pull him over. My right hand is still hooked onto his left arm, and I am using my left hand to apply pressure to his leg and take it out from underneath him.

8 As I complete my roll, I land in the armlock position. I cross my left foot over the top of my right, which is very important. If I crossed my right foot over my left, it would create space for my brother to lift his right shoulder. I want to hold his shoulder down using my right leg, and crossing my left foot over my right gives me the best leverage. Letting the crook of my right arm slide up to his wrist, I arch my hips and finish the submission. Notice how I haven't let go of his left leg with my left arm—this absolutely kills his defense.

HIGH FIREMAN'S CARRY TO ARMLOCK

A lot of wrestlers and jiu-jitsu practitioners will attempt to throw you with a high fireman's carry, especially the big boys who like to manhandle their opponents with strength. But the process of picking you up and then bringing you back down can take an ample amount of time, and you can use that time to maneuver around your opponent and assume an armlock position. I have caught a lot of heavyweights with this technique.

1 My brother and I are squared off, searching for an opening.

2 As my brother reaches to grab, a gut feeling tells me that he will try to pull me in and lift me up.

3 My brother reaches in and squats down to lift me off my feet. As he does this, I wrap my right hand around his left arm and cup just behind his elbow.

4 As my brother lifts me off my feet, I post my left hand on his hip. This will help me throw my left leg around to the front of his left leg in the next move. I also kick my right foot in a clockwise direction to lock his right arm in place.

5 I throw my left leg around to the front of my brother's left leg. Here I have him in the standard armlock position; the only difference is my brother is standing up.

6 As my brother drops me down, I wrap my left hand around his left leg and pull my body close. This will make it harder for him to remain in the standing position. I also cross my feet, locking me really tight to his body.

7 As my head comes down between my brother's legs, I continue to control his left leg with my left arm. Because my head and weight is centered between his legs, it makes it particularly hard for him to remain standing.

8   Using my left hand, I pull my brother's leg out front underneath him as he starts to roll forward. I also bridge my body to help aid the roll.

9   My feet remain crossed as my brother rolls onto his upper back. Notice that I have the same armlock position as I did when my brother was standing. I have his left arm hooked in the crook of my right arm, and I continue to hold onto his left leg with my right arm.

10   With my left foot still crossed over my right, I apply downward pressure with my knees, giving me the leverage to straighten my brother's arm and finish the submission.

TOMOE-NAGE ARMLOCK

When you drop to your back to execute a tomoe-nage, your opponent will often counter the throw by posting his arms. Although this eliminates the two points you would have earned on the judges' scorecards, it opens up a submission opportunity. With your opponent's arms straight, you can reposition his body into the armlock position using your feet. My brother is an absolute master at this technique, and he has used it to finish many opponents in jiu-jitsu competition.

1 I have a standard sleeve and collar grip, preparing to execute a tomoe-nage.

2 I step forward with my right foot.

3 Pulling down with my grips, I rotate my hips slightly in a counterclockwise direction and lift my left foot to plant it on my brother's belt-line.

4 As I plant my left foot on my brother's belt-line, I continue to rotate in a counterclockwise direction toward my left side. As I do this, I bend my right knee and edge my hips toward the gap between his legs. Notice that the toes and heel of my right foot run straight along my brother's belt. If I hadn't rotated slightly in a counterclockwise direction, this positioning would be hard to achieve.

5 As I drop into a backwards roll, I pull my grips toward my head almost as if I am trying to put on a big hat. My right foot is planted on the ground for stability, and I apply upward pressure into my brother's belt with my left foot to lift him off the ground and cast him into the throw.

6 I have my brother up in the air. Notice that my left hand is controlling his elbow and my right hand is controlling his collar—perfect for the armlock position.

7 My brother has locked his arms to resist the throw. Instead of sticking with my original plan, which will score me two points at best, I decide to drop my brother's body into the armlock position and go for the submission. My left foot is already on the right side of his belt, toes pointing out. Now I put my right foot on the left side of his belt, toes also pointing out. So my heels have come close together and my feet are forming a V.

8 I rotate my brother's body above me by dropping my left foot and pushing up with my right foot. Notice how this causes his entire body to turn.

9 My brother lands in the armlock position. I throw my left leg over his head, cross my feet, and secure his right arm in the crook of my left arm.

10 As I drop back, I let the crook of my left arm slide up to his wrist. Crossing my right hand over the top of my left wrist for added control and pressure, I pull his arm to my chest and arch my hips, locking in the submission.

WALK PAST GUARD

If you chuck an opponent in competition with one of the judo techniques you have learned, the chances are he will be very hesitant to engage if the fight gets stood back up. There is a good possibility that he will try to avoid your stand-up altogether by jumping guard. This shouldn't worry you too much because a lot of jiu-jitsu practitioners jump guard improperly, even black belts. As a matter of fact, many of them don't even jump guard—they just sit down into it. If you time it right and have good control, you can use this technique to walk right past your opponent's guard and assume the standard impact control position. If you get caught in your opponent's guard, then you deal with it. But this is an excellent way to bypass that entire process and stay aggressive.

1 Pretending to be a jiu-jitsu practitioner with no judo training, my brother assumes a low jiu-jitsu stance.

2 I establish a standard sleeve and collar grip and use them to stand my brother up just enough to set up a throw.

3 My brother steps his left leg forward. Because he is a strict jiu-jitsu practitioner, he is not quick with his movement. I know he is either trying to attack with a throw or sit down to his guard. I assume it is the latter.

4 As my brother sits to pull guard, I quickly pull his upper body up toward me using my grips. At the same time, I step my right leg over the top of his right leg.

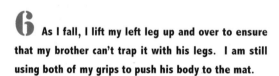

5 Now that my right leg is over his right leg, I use my grips to push my brother's body down to the mat. I am going to fall with him to ensure that he doesn't try to reestablish the guard position.

6 As I fall, I lift my left leg up and over to ensure that my brother can't trap it with his legs. I am still using both of my grips to push his body to the mat.

7 I land in the standard impact control position, ready to transition into a submission.

BLOCK GUARD WITH KNEE

When your opponent jumps guard, he is usually trying to wrap you up in his closed guard. Utilizing this technique is a good way to disrupt his game plan. It stops your opponent from being able to wrap his legs around you, which allows you to transition to the impact control position. The previous technique is best because you bypass your opponent's guard entirely, but it is important to always have a backup.

1 Here my brother and I both have a sleeve and collar grip. Not comfortable standing with me because of my judo background, my brother immediately tries to jump guard. The moment he lifts his left leg to jump, I raise my right knee and dig my shin between his legs on the left side of his groin. To ensure that my leg gets deep, I use my grips to slightly arch my back and thrust my knee forward.

2 As my brother rolls to his back, my positioning forces his legs to spread. Because I lifted my right knee, my right shin comes down onto his leg and traps it to the ground, preventing him from pulling me into his closed guard. I also have my left knee up, which keeps my brother's right leg far away from his left. From here I will keep his left leg pinned as I rotate my left leg in a counterclockwise direction so it clears his right leg. Then I can assume the standard impact control position.

ANTI-JUDO

Whether you are grappling in a Judo match, a jiu-jitsu competition, or an MMA bout, the rules of the event will dictate behavior. Judo players hate to get mounted because in judo that is considered a pin, and a pin means the end of the match. After you throw a judoka, he will usually turn over and ball up on all fours, giving you his back. It is considered by jiu-jitsu players to be an extremely vulnerable position, but because judo players spend so much time in this position during practice, it can be hard to catch them in a submission. They become like a turtle hiding in his shell. Instead of attacking a judo player while he is in his balled up shell, I have learned that it is much more efficient to pull him out of his shell first. I achieve that by employing this technique. It forces my opponent to roll over onto his back. Fearful of getting pinned and losing the match, he will try desperately to get back to all fours, exposing his arms in the process. That is when I go for the armlock. Although this move is designed to play upon my fellow judo players' fear of the judo pin, it works just as good in jiu-jitsu competition against an opponent who is quick to give his back and difficult to sprawl out.

1 Having lost my grips after throwing my brother, he quickly rolled over and balled up on all fours to keep me from pinning him to the mat and winning the match.

2 Planting my right knee on my brother's lower back, I slide my left leg across his belt-line and hook my foot around his right thigh. I could attempt a chokehold from this position, but because my brother is a skilled judoka, I know that his choke defense is strong.

3 With my left foot still hooked around my brother's right thigh, I post my right foot on his right side. Then I drop my right hand and grip his sleeve.

4 Rotating my upper body slightly in a counterclockwise direction, I move my right elbow to the left side of my brother's head.

5 I drive my right elbow into the left side of my brother's head.

6 I cock my right leg back to generate the momentum needed to roll my brother over.

7 Using my right elbow pressed against the left side of my brother's head as leverage, I kick my right leg in a counterclockwise direction toward his head. At the same time, I drop my right shoulder toward my left hand. Because I still have my left leg hooked underneath my brother, I force him to roll with me. Notice how I still have my grip on his sleeve. This will keep him from posting his right arm and stopping the roll.

8 Because of the momentum and leverage I generated with my movements, I dump my brother over onto his right shoulder, basically forcing him into a shoulder roll. My right knee plants on the mat, but I keep my left foot arched around his right leg, hindering him from posting his knee and stopping the roll.

9 As my brother lands, my left hand is still posted on the mat and I still have my right grip on his sleeve. Not wanting to get pinned, this is where my brother freaks out. He wants to get back to his knees, but the moment he turns away from me to achieve this, I pull up on his sleeve with my right hand and drive my right elbow down into his head. This limits his leverage, making it very difficult for him to get back to his knees and his turtle shell.

10 Because my brother can't turn away from me and get back to his knees, he turns into me. While he is still focused on getting back to his knees, I pull up with my sleeve grip to straighten his arm. The more he turns, the straighter his arm gets. Notice how I have kept my right arm tight against my body. This will hinder my brother from dropping his right shoulder to the ground if he realizes he's fallen into a trap.

11 Rotating my body in a clockwise direction, I use my grip to pull my brother's right arm toward his legs. At the same time, I plant my left hand on his head and push down so I can easily throw my leg over.

12 Stepping my left leg over my brother's head, I wrap the crook of my left arm around his right arm, setting up the armlock. By focusing on getting to his knees, my brother has put himself in this predicament.

13 I drop back, pull my brother's arm to my chest, squeeze my knees together, and arch my hips. Notice that I am still gripping my brother's sleeve with my right hand. That hasn't changed since the beginning of the move. If I had tried to change my grip, I would have lost all the leverage I gained through my movements.

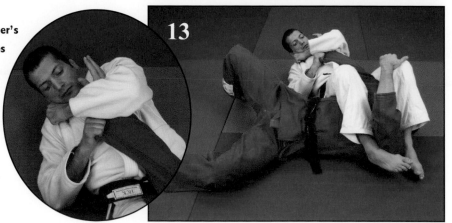

SECTION THREE

FLYING ATTACKS

FLYING ATTACKS

Before attempting flying attacks you must be extremely comfortable with falling. If you are not comfortable with falling, you will not be able to focus on your movements while in the air, which makes the possibility for injury greater. It is also important that you understand the basic submissions. You should have drilled them on the ground thousands of times because that will be the same movement you execute five feet off the ground. If you've read and studied this book from the start, none of this should be an issue. You started by acquiring basic rolling techniques, moved onto light throws, and then developed the ability to land and break your fall when thrown hard. You've learned what it is like to get propelled into the air, and now you are just going to go a little higher. For most flying attacks, the majority of your body will be above your opponent's shoulders. Since you already know how to break your fall by impacting with your elbows first, this shouldn't be a concern. This is where the thousands of simple rolls you practiced at the beginning of each training session will come in handy.

You might be asking yourself right now, 'Why should I learn how to do flying attacks? They look pretty cool, but I rarely see one end a match.' The reason you don't see flying attacks in competition is because people don't know how to do them properly. Back in the beginning of my jiu-jitsu career, I saw a fighter flying armlock one of Frank Shamrock's guys. I thought it was the coolest move ever, but I blew the technique off because I didn't think it would be applicable a large percentage of the time. Then a year or so later I attended a seminar being given by Oleg Taktarov, and he was teaching how to do flying armlocks. I still thought it was a cool, but I realized my initial feelings were right. They were being taught from a standard armlock position in the air, which made them very hard to apply in a real fight because your opponent could easily counter by facing you and grabbing onto your leg. But the whole art of flying up and attacking your opponent made a serious impact on me, and I decided to devote some time to making them work. Over the next half a decade, as I moved up through the belts, I changed the way flying attacks were done. Instead of jumping up into the standard armlock position, I jumped up into a triangle position. I did this by smashing my leg down between my opponent's shoulder and head. This would not only discombobulate him, but also straighten his arm into the triangle position. I could then use that positioning to transition to the armlock position. Understanding this, I changed the existing techniques so that they would work a large percentage of the time. I also developed a host of new flying attacks that worked an even larger percentage of the time.

When I started submitting my opponents with flying attacks as a purple belt, I knew I was onto something. My opponents seldom saw them coming, and they had no idea how to defend against them. I continued to do them as much as possible in both judo and jiu-jitsu matches, and soon no one wanted anything to do with my stand-up. Every time I squared off with an opponent, he would keep his elbows locked tight against his body. Although that made flying attacks rather difficult, it cut down on my opponent's offense, which opened up other opportunities. Eventually my opponents resorted to jumping guard. I liked the feeling of scaring my opponents with my presence. I wanted all my students to experience those same feelings, so I've been teaching them flying attacks for several years now. The following techniques are not rocket science. I have a fifteen-year-old blue belt who lands them left and right in practice. If you've done all your homework up to this point, they should come naturally.

CRASH PAD SAFETY

When first starting out with flying attacks, it is mandatory that you take precautionary measures. The best way to do that is by only practicing flying attacks on thick, heavy mats. I recommend Swain mats. They are about a foot thick, and they will absorb most of your fall if you should slip off your opponent's shoulders or land in an awkward position. Once you crash down on them a few times, you'll realize how soft they are and lose your fear of falling. This will maximize your learning potential while at the same time limit the potential for injury.

1 Get one of these Swain mats to serve as your crash pad. They stand about eight inches off the normal mat, and they are very soft.

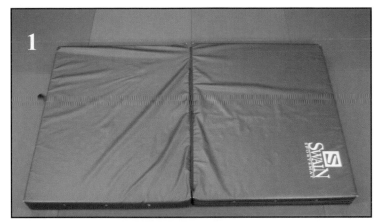

2 Standing on the Swain mat, I'm preparing to break a backward fall. You can see how the mat gives where I am stepping on it.

3 Instead of crouching and rolling backwards as I did on the normal mats, here I am pushing off with my right leg and jumping into the air. As I get closer to the mat, my elbows will drop below my body so they impact first and break my fall.

4 As I land, my elbows break my fall. Notice how my knees are up and my chin is tucked. I just ate ten minutes before executing this move, and I feel fine.

TRIANGLE ARMLOCK DEMONSTRATION

To execute a flying attack you must assume the triangle position in the air. However, before attempting this it is important that you drill proper technique over and over on the ground so the triangle position becomes instinctual. If you have this technique down and you are used to landing on the crash pad, you should be ready for flying attacks.

1 I have my brother trapped between my legs in my closed guard. My hands are on his sleeves, controlling his elbows.

2 Using my left sleeve grip on my brother's right elbow to pull his arm toward me, I place my right hand above my left to further control his arm. Then I throw my right leg over his arm and crash the crook of my leg down between his shoulder and neck. As I do this, I place my left foot on my brother's right hip.

3 I throw my left leg over to the left side of my brother's head and cross it over my right shin. Pinching my knees together and continuing to pull his arm toward me, I set myself up for the armlock.

4 With my right hand still controlling above my brother's elbow, which keeps him from pulling his arm free, I slide the crook of my left arm up to his wrist, which hinders him from wriggling his arm from side to side.

5 I double up on my brother's wrist. As I drive my elbows into my body for added pressure, I arch my hips and lock in the submission.

TRIANGLE EFFICIENCY

Here I am showing the right way and the wrong way to throw your leg over your opponent's head to assume the triangle position. It is a very simple concept—keep your leg as close to your opponent's head as possible—but many jiu-jitsu practitioners make a big loop with their leg and lose the submission as a result. The farther your leg strays from your opponent's head, the more time and opportunity he will have to counter. It would be the same as a boxer throwing a huge, looping punch, giving his adversary plenty of time to duck or throw a bomb straight down the pipe.

1 I'm right about to throw my leg over my brother's head and finish the armlock.

2 Notice how I am skimming my left leg across the right side of my brother's head as I throw it over. This is the right way to make the transition.

3 I clamp down and finish the submission.

4 This is the way I see some jiu-jitsu practitioners set up the transition to throw their leg over. Notice how my left knee is far away from my brother's body. Here my brother can pull his arm out and escape. You never want to do it this way.

5 This is the wrong way to sweep your leg around. Notice that there is even more space between my left leg and my brother's body. Now it is very easy for my brother to escape, especially if he uses all his strength. If you keep your leg close to your opponent's head, the likelihood of his escape is a lot less.

6 I finish just as I did before, but I took unnecessary risk to get here.

FLYING TRIANGLE TO ARMLOCK

When executing this technique, the second your opponent reaches you want to gain control of one of his elbows and then fly into action. It works just as well on an opponent who is hunched over as it does on an opponent who is standing erect, making it a versatile submission. And when you come down your body is already bridged, making it extremely hard for your opponent to stack you by dropping his weight. There are, however, things to look out for. If your opponent manages to get two grips on your gi before you launch into the attack, it can be hard to secure the triangle position in the air. In that case, you might want to utilize a traditional flying armlock, but it usually won't work as well as this one. If you are like me, this will become your bread and butter of flying attacks.

1 My brother and I are squared off. I have an assortment of flying attacks at the ready, searching for an opening to launch into one.

2 As my brother reaches his right hand forward to assume a grip on my collar, I acquire a sleeve grip just above his elbow. At the same time, I obtain a collar grip and place my left foot on his right hip to gain the leverage needed to launch into my flying attack.

3 As I explode upward off both feet, I use my right grip on my brother's collar to pull my body towards him and help gain height for my attack. Notice that my right leg is bent as it comes off the ground. I am going to raise it up on the outside of my brother's left shoulder, and then crash it down between his shoulder and neck. The impact will stun him and make it harder for him to defend my attack.

4 My right leg has come up and over my brother's shoulder, and now I'm crashing it down between his shoulder and neck. I'm still pulling myself toward my brother with my right collar grip, causing him to fall forward.

5 Because I am still gripping my brother's gi, pulling my body into him, I come down to the mat with very little force. As a matter of fact, in this photo I am actually suspended a few inches off the mat, hanging off my brother. My hips are already bridged here, so even if my brother tries to drop his weight, it will be very difficult for him to stack me.

6 I throw my left leg over my brother's head and cross it over the top of my right shin. Sometimes I do this even before I hit the ground. Now that I'm in the triangle position, I can finish the armlock. It is important on this technique not to cut your jump short because then your hips will not end up snug against your opponent. Notice here how tight I am with my brother. I caught a guy in this move during a competition, and he decided to stand up and walk around—I just dangled off of him like a tree branch. If you are not tight, your opponent will have the ability to shake you off his arm.

ELBOW CONTROL FLYING ARMLOCK

This is essentially the same technique as the previous one, except here you have secured a high grip. This is a great move to use when your opponent reaches in for a high grip and you intercept it. While your opponent is still thinking about grip fighting, you are moving into a flying attack. I've caught many people off guard with this one.

1 My brother and I are squared off with our opposite feet forward.

2 My brother reaches in with his right hand to assume a high grip, and I block it with my left hand, coiling my fingers around his arm just above his elbow.

3 I scoop my left hand around my brother's arm and then bring my elbow to my body, locking his arm tight. Notice my fingers are gripping his gi just above his elbow.

4 Now that I have my grip and control my brother's right elbow, I immediately make my move before my brother can get his second grip. As I punch my right arm forward and assume a high grip, I push off with my left foot. Notice how my right foot is already starting to leave the mat.

5 Pushing off with my left foot and pulling my body up and into my brother with my high grip, I kick my right foot up and over his shoulder.

6 As I crash my right leg down between my brother's left shoulder and head, my weight begins to drop back and it pulls my brother down. Notice that I am still latched onto my brother with my grips, making me a part of his body.

7 As I land, I throw my left leg over my brother's head and cross it over the top of my right. Already bridging my hips, it makes it difficult for my brother to drive his weight down and stack me. Releasing my left grip on his sleeve, I let the crook of my left arm slide up to his wrist. I then let go of the high grip and cross my right arm over the top of my left wrist for added leverage. To finish the armlock, I pull my elbows into my body to straighten my brother's arm and arch my hips forward.

SHOULDER GRIP FLYING ARMLOCK

This is a flying armlock off a shoulder grip. I used this technique at the Senior Nationals when my opponent established a grip with his right hand and then kept his entire right side dramatically forward in an attempt to protect his left side. He achieved his goal of protecting his left side, but in the process he got caught in a flying armlock. The entire match lasted five seconds.

1 My brother and I are both in extreme stances. He is extreme right because his right shoulder his dramatically forward, and I am extreme left because my left shoulder is dramatically forward. Notice that our lead feet are almost touching.

2 As my brother reaches forward to assume a collar grip, I intercept it by latching onto his sleeve with my right hand. At the same time, I reach my left arm forward and establish a grip on his shoulder. From here I am going to use my right grip to keep his arm straight and my left grip to generate leverage to jump into my flying attack.

3 The second I establish my grips I place my left foot on my brother's hip. Notice how I'm coiling my right hand into my body to keep his arm straight and using my left to pull myself up.

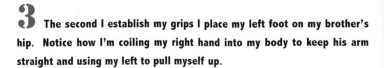

4 Pushing off with my left foot and pulling up with my left hand, I kick my right leg up and over my brother's shoulder.

5 After crashing my right leg down between my brother's shoulder and neck, my weight drops back. This forces my brother to lean forward and I get gently lowered to the mat. My right hand is still controlling his sleeve, and I still have my left grip on his shoulder.

6 Although I haven't yet come down to the mat, I throw my left leg over my brother's head and cross it over my right leg. Pinching my knees together to trap his arm, I let go of my shoulder grip and slide the crook of my left arm down to my brother's right wrist. I finish the submission while still off the mat by pulling his arm to my chest with my left elbow, pinching my knees together, and arching my hips.

FLYING TRIANGLE

Sometimes it can be difficult to straighten your opponent's arm while squared off in the standing position. This should make you very cautious about heading into a flying attack, but if your opponent's elbow is away from his body and it feels right, you can use a flying attack to establish the triangle position. Once you come down onto the mat, you can then finish him with the triangle.

1 My brother and I both have extreme stances. Notice that we have opposite feet forward, resulting in our lead feet being close together.

2 My brother goes for the high grip and I intercept it with my left hand. Immediately I notice that he is leaning forward, his elbow is away from his body, and his left hand is low. Even through I haven't straightened out his right arm, everything is screaming for me to launch into a flying triangle.

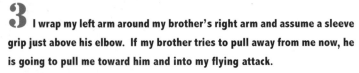

3 I wrap my left arm around my brother's right arm and assume a sleeve grip just above his elbow. If my brother tries to pull away from me now, he is going to pull me toward him and into my flying attack.

4 I punch my right hand forward and assume a high grip on my brother's left side. Although I am showing this in steps, it is important to remember that all flying attacks are explosive. The moment you get your grips, you launch into your attack.

5 Pushing off the ground with my left foot and pulling my body up with my high grip, I lift my right leg and crash it down between my brother's shoulder and neck.

6 As my right leg crashes down between my brother's shoulder and neck, my weight falls backwards and forces him to slowly lower me to the mat. The trick with this move is to shoot your crotch all the way up into your opponent's armpit while your head is dropping back. It will force your opponent to lean over, making it very hard for him to defend your attack.

7 I land in the trap triangle position.

8 Letting go of my high grip and bridging my hips, I use my right hand to pull my brother's arm across my body. Notice that I still have my left sleeve grip above his elbow. It is also important to notice that I am not reaching up to grab my foot as many jiu-jitsu practitioners would do in this situation.

9 Now that I have his arm across my body, I pull my brother down using my legs. I have still not reached up and grabbed my foot. When people try to make the transition between closed guard and the triangle position, the number one reason their opponents escape is because they try to reach up and grab their foot for leverage. Notice here that I can pull my brother down just fine using my closed guard. With his arm buried on my right side, he is not going anywhere.

10 Instead of opening my guard to try and secure the triangle position, I reach up and grab my right shin to form the triangle between my right leg and left arm. In my opinion, everyone should change their triangles to this method. This is how they are most effective—using the shin and not the foot. The foot is too far away, and my left knee is in the way, making it hard to grab.

11 I wrap the crook of my left leg over my right foot to secure everything. Notice that my left hand still hasn't left my shin. My brother is as good as done here.

12 Using my left hand on my shin as leverage, I press my left elbow into my brother's head. I reach my right hand up and grab my knee to apply additional downward pressure. To finish the submission, I squeeze my elbows and knees together. In a matter of seconds my brother will be sleeping.

FLYING TRIANGLE TO OMOPLATA

This is an excellent flying attack to employ when your opponent shoots in for a single leg takedown. While he is focused on bringing the fight to the ground, you launch into the normal flying triangle position and then finish with an Omoplata. It can be a very deceptive move when done with proper speed and technique.

1 My brother and I are squared off with opposite feet forward.

2 My brother shoots in for a single leg takedown. To redirect some of his forward momentum, I place my left hand on his head and push it down toward his right foot. At the same time, I drop my right hand to establish a sleeve grip above his left elbow. If he drives in hard, I will hop away to maintain balance.

3 As my brother lifts my right leg, I continue to push his head down and away with my left hand. I also establish a sleeve grip above his elbow with my right hand. Notice here how I'm pointing the toes of my right foot to the floor so I can move my foot around his left knee and to the outside of his leg.

4 I place my right foot on the outside of my brother's left leg.

5 Cupping my left hand around the back of my brother's neck and using my right grip to pull my body up into him, I generate additional leverage to spring off my left foot.

6 I crash my left leg down between my brother's neck and shoulder, and then I cross my feet. As my weight drops backwards, I cling onto his neck with my left hand and his left elbow with my right grip. Notice how my dropping weight pulls my brother's body forward.

7 As my body comes down onto the mat, I place my left hand on the side of his head and push it away. This will give me room to throw my left leg over to the left side of his head. Notice how his left arm is still hooked around my leg from his takedown attempt, and how I'm using my right grip to keep it locked in place.

8 Still pushing my brother's head away with my left hand, I throw my left leg over to the left side of his head.

9 Crossing my left foot over my right, I put downward pressure on my brother's left shoulder, which drives his face toward the mat. Notice how I have moved my left hand to his shoulder to lock his arm in place and reached my right hand up for a high grip on his belt.

10 With my brother's face down on the mat, I post my left arm and use it along with my grip on his belt to sit up.

11 As I sit up, I grab the back of my brother's collar with my left hand. This helps me sit up even more, putting tremendous pressure on my brother's left shoulder and causing him to tap in submission.

OPTION FOR FLYING OMOPLATA #1

This is a good technique to use when your opponent establishes a grip on your collar. You're going to break his grip, redirect it, and then throw a leg over his shoulder. If your opponent doesn't fight your movement, then you can finish the battle with the omoplata submission. Sometimes it is just that easy, and other times your opponent will be more aggressive in his defense. As you will see in the upcoming moves, you have a number of different options once you have your leg over. Deciding which submission to utilize depends upon your opponent's reactions.

1 My brother and I are squared off. Unlike in the previous technique, we have the same foot forward.

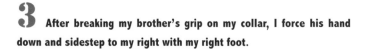

2 My brother establishes a collar grip with his left hand, and I reach up to establish a sleeve grip on both sides of his wrist with my hands. Now I am going to use the "Breaking the Collar Grip" technique described in the first section to force his hand down.

3 After breaking my brother's grip on my collar, I force his hand down and sidestep to my right with my right foot.

4 Pulling my brother's left arm straight with my right sleeve grip so he can't use it to defend, I plant my left hand on the side of his head and push it away, further separating his arm from his body.

5 After a quick push off with my right foot, I throw my right leg over my brother's back. This is where my brother will react to my movement, and I will choose my submission in accordance with his reactions. In this particular case, my brother is still trying to figure out what is going on, so his reactions are minimal. As a result, I'm going to finish him with the omoplata.

6 Pulling my brother's left arm up with my sleeve grip, I wrap the crook of my right leg around his left arm. To secure his arm away from his body and lock everything down, I grab the shin of my right leg with my left hand.

7 Establishing a grip on the right side of my brother's back with my right hand, I hop my left foot back and drive my weight down into his left shoulder, forcing my brother to collapse to his knees and right arm.

8 As my brother comes down, I use my right grip on his back and my left grip on my shin to drive my hips forward into his arm, putting tremendous pressure on my brother's shoulder and causing him to tap in submission.

OPTION FOR FLYING OMOPLATA #2

In the previous technique you threw your leg over your opponent's back and forced his head down to finish with the omoplata. In this situation, your opponent lifts his head the moment you throw your leg over. Although this hinders you from getting the omoplata, it sets you up perfectly for a flying triangle. With all of your opponent's attention focused on raising his head, he most likely won't see this move coming.

1 My brother and I are squared off with the same foot forward.

2 Just as with the previous technique, my brother establishes a collar grip with his left hand. I reach up to establish a sleeve grip on both sides of his wrist with my hands. Now I am going to use the "Breaking the Collar Grip" technique described in the first section to force his hand down.

3 After breaking my brother's grip on my collar, I force his hand down and sidestep to my right with my right foot.

4 Pulling my brother's left arm straight with my right sleeve grip so he can't use it to defend, I plant my left hand on the side of his head and push it away, further separating his arm from his body.

5 After a quick push off with my right foot, I throw my right leg over my brother's back.

6-7 Just as I was about to wrap the crook of my right leg around my brother's left arm, he starts raising his head. In a split second, I abandon the omoplata and decide to transition to a flying triangle. I start the technique by assuming a high grip on his collar with my left hand, and then using that grip to pull myself up and into him as I jump off my left foot.

8 After crashing my left leg down between my brother's right shoulder and neck, my weight causes my brother to slowly lower my body to the ground. Notice that as I come down, my feet come together and I cross my left foot over my right. I still have my left collar grip, and I'm still controlling my brother's left arm with my right sleeve grip. I have a closed guard and the triangle position.

9 I hook my left hand around my brother's right heel, and I use that hook to rotate my body in a clockwise direction, giving me the angle needed to attack his arm. Notice that I'm still controlling my brother's left arm at the elbow, and that his wrist is trapped between my right elbow and side. I am also pinching my knees together to keep him from pulling his head and arm out of the triangle position.

10 Continuing to use my left hook around my brother's right leg, I complete my clockwise rotation and assume the proper angle needed to attack his arm. I throw my right leg over to the right side of my brother's head and cross my right foot over my left. Applying downward pressure to his left arm with my right elbow, I hyperextend his arm, causing him to tap in submission.

OPTION FOR FLYING OMOPLATA #3

In this situation your opponent pulls his trapped arm free when you throw your leg over, totally escaping the omoplata. To deal with the new development, you're going to jump onto his back, force him to the mat, and then end with a choke. You should spend some time nailing this one down because a lot of opponents will react to the omoplata by yanking their arm free. As long as you are quick to counter their defense, you will still end the battle with a submission.

1 My brother and I are squared off with the same foot forward.

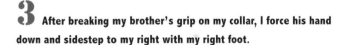

2 Just as with the previous technique, my brother establishes a collar grip with his left hand. I reach up to establish a sleeve grip on both sides of his wrist with my hands. Now I am going to use the "Breaking the Collar Grip" technique described in the first section to force his hand down.

3 After breaking my brother's grip on my collar, I force his hand down and sidestep to my right with my right foot.

4 Pulling my brother's left arm straight with my right sleeve grip so he can't use it to defend, I plant my left hand on the side of his head and push it away, further separating his arm from his body.

5 After a quick push off with my right foot, I throw my right leg over my brother's back.

6 I wrap the crook of my right leg around my brother's left arm. Before I can grab my right shin with my hand to trap his arm, he starts pulling his arm free.

7 My brother pulls his arm totally free. Realizing I have lost the omoplata, I throw my right leg over his back and continue to bar his head.

8 I jump onto my brother's back. As I do this, I wrap my right forearm across his throat and establish a collar grip with my right hand. Notice how I am using my left hand to feed by brother's collar into my right hand for a better grip.

9 With my right hand tightly gripping my brother's left collar, I slide off my brother's back toward my left shoulder. As I do this, I hook my left arm around my brother's left leg. I will keep rotating until my brother comes with me. With his collar already digging into his throat, he can't offer much resistance.

10 As I roll down onto my left shoulder, my brother comes with me. My left arm is still hooked around his left leg.

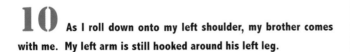

11 As my brother lands, I throw my right leg over his right shoulder. I also cross my left foot over the top of my right. I still have my left arm hooked around his left leg, and now I latch my left hand onto my collar to keep him from freeing his leg. With his shoulders pinned and his left leg trapped, it is very difficult for my brother to move. Pulling with my right hand, I dig my brother's collar deep into his throat and he taps in submission.

FLYING REVERSE TRIANGLE

When you jump up for a flying attack, sometimes you'll notice that your opponent is slightly bent over with his head angled down. In such a situation, you can actually sit down on his shoulders and spin your body around his head to finish with a triangle. It is quite possible for your opponent to straighten his posture when you launch yourself at him, so this is not a move you want to head into directly from your feet. You will realize once you're in the air how your opponent is reacting, and if he remains bent over with his head down, you can then abandon your initial flying attack and transition to the flying reverse triangle. It is a tricky move, but it works great under the right circumstance.

1 My brother and I are squared up with opposite feet forward.

2 My brother reaches in for a collar grip, and I instantly control his right elbow with a sleeve grip.

3 Punching my right hand in for a high grip, I use both of my grips to pull myself up and into my brother as I plant my left foot on his hip.

4 While in mid-air I notice that my brother is in somewhat of a squat position. Because I have the height, I make the decision to rotate by body around his head and finish with a triangle. So instead of crashing my right leg down between his shoulder and head and letting my weight drop back, I sit down on his left shoulder and continue to rotate my body in a counterclockwise direction.

5 To rotate in a counterclockwise direction around my brother's head, I use my grips and push off my brother's hip with my left foot.

6 As I complete my rotation around my brother's head, I reach down and grab my left shin with my right hand. Notice how I am using my sleeve grip to pull up on his elbow. This allows me to slip my left leg underneath his arm. Here I am already locked into the triangle position, ready to drop my weight into a forward roll.

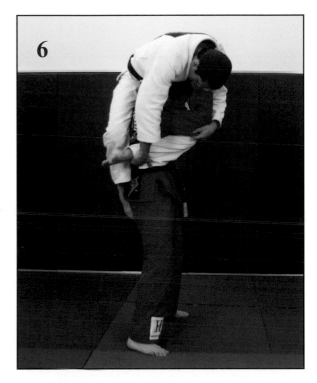

7 As my head drops between my brother's legs into a forward roll, I hook my right leg over my left foot. My brother and I are now locked together—where I go, he goes.

8 As my head comes down to the mat between my brother's legs, I already have the triangle locked in. I still have a lot of momentum with my lower body, and because my brother is attached to my lower body, he has no choice but to get carried over to his back.

9 As my brother's body gets carried over into the roll, I reach my right arm up and hook it around his right leg. This will help me control his roll.

10 My brother lands on his back in the triangle position. I bridge my hips and pull his right leg toward my body to lock everything tight.

11 As I fall over to my left side, I hook the crook of my left arm around my brother's ankle and hook my right hand around the back of his knee. To lock in the submission, I tighten the crook of my right leg over my left foot, pull my brother's leg into my body, and arch my hips forward. If my brother does not tap, he will go to sleep.

FLYING ARMLOCK FROM WIZARD

This technique comes in handy when your opponent hooks one of your arms and tries to get you in a standing armlock. Instead of fighting the armlock, you go with it, increasing your opponent's confidence. As he puts all of his focus into the submission, you bar his head and move directly into your flying attack, catching him completely off guard.

1 My brother and I are squared off with the same foot forward.

2 As I reach for my brother's collar, he hooks his left arm over the top of my right arm.

3-4 While I am trying to establish an under-hook, my brother angles his fist to the ground and drives the crook of his arm down into my elbow. When I don't pull my arm free, my brother sees a chance to end the fight with a submission and really starts cranking on my arm.

5 As my brother focuses on his armlock, I post my right hand on the back of his head and push it down toward his right foot.

6 With my brother's head no longer in the way, I push off with my right foot and throw my left knee over his right shoulder. Notice that I still have my right arm hooked underneath my brother's left arm.

7 With my left leg now behind my brother's head, my right leg comes up and hooks around the front of my brother's face. Notice that I still have my right arm hooked underneath my brother's left arm.

8 Rotating my body in a clockwise direction, my head starts to come down between my brother's knees. I still have my right arm hooked around my brother's left arm, and my right leg is hooked around the right side of his head.

9 I pull my brother's arm toward my chest with my right arm as I come down onto my shoulders between his legs. My right leg is still hooked around his head, and I drop my left knee and dig my shin into his side. I also hook my left arm around my brother's left foot.

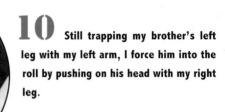

10 Still trapping my brother's left leg with my left arm, I force him into the roll by pushing on his head with my right leg.

11 As my brother's body goes over, I continue to trap his left leg with my left arm and his right arm with my right arm.

12 My brother lands in the armlock position. I let the crook my left arm slide up to the back of his left knee for control. To lock in the submission, I pull his arm to my chest with my right arm, pinch my knees together, and arch my hips upward.

FLYING ARM-DRAG TO BACK

In this technique you'll be executing an arm-drag from the standing position, jumping to guard, taking your opponent's back, and then sweeping out one of your opponent's legs to land in a mount position with a choke. If done with speed and proper technique, your opponent will become overwhelmed by the number of moves and have a very hard time defending.

1 My brother and I are squared off with the same foot forward.

2 As my brother reaches his left arm forward to establish a grip, I intercept it with my right hand, establish a sleeve grip, and then drag his arm toward my left side.

3 Using my right grip to pull my brother's arm to my left, I reach my left arm forward and establish a grip just above his elbow. Then I use both grips to drag his arm to my left.

4 I step my right foot to the outside of my brother's left leg as I drag his arm past my chest to my left. Because my brother's left arm is away from his body, he is weak on his left side.

5 Before my brother has a chance to pull his arm back and recover, I reach my right arm over his back to establish a grip on his right side. I then use that grip to pull myself in a counterclockwise direction as I throw my left leg across the front of his hips. My left hand is still pulling on the arm drag.

6 I throw my right leg over my brother's back and wrap my right foot over the top of my left foot, putting me in a standing side guard position. I release my right grip on my brother's back and reach my right hand over his shoulder to establish a grip on his left collar. It is important to grab the left collar because that is what you will use to apply the choke. As my body lowers toward the mat, I release my left sleeve grip and hook my left arm around the back of his left leg.

7 Still with a closed guard on the left side of my brother's body, my right hand starts applying pressure to the choke. I still have my left arm hooked around my brother's left leg, but now I also latch onto his left sleeve with my left hand. It is very difficult for my brother to move in this position.

8 Continuing into my shoulder roll, my brother has no choice but to come down with me. Notice that I have maintained a closed side guard by keeping my feet crossed. I am also still applying pressure to the choke with my right grip on his collar.

9 As my brother lands, I uncross my feet so I can throw my right leg over his right shoulder. I still have his left leg trapped with my left arm and I'm applying pressure to the choke with my right grip.

10 My right leg comes over my brother's shoulder, and then I cross my left foot over my right. I finish the choke by straightening my right arm and pulling my shoulder away.

DEALING WITH FLYING ATTACK DEFENSE OPTION #1

Sometimes when you jump into a flying attack, your opponent will defend by thrusting his hips forward. This helps him stay standing, which can make it difficult for you to gain the leverage needed to secure the armlock. Most people will abandon their flying attack in this situation, but that doesn't have to be the case. As long as you maintain good elbow control, you can dangle off of your opponent, do some repositioning, and finish with an omoplata, a triangle, or an armlock. It can be extremely beneficial to practice this by hanging off a training partner and attempting to apply one of the three following techniques while he is defending.

1 I have a standard sleeve grip above my brother's elbow.

2 I reach my right hand forward and establish a grip on my brother's right collar.

3 I jump up to assume the standard flying triangle position.

4 I land in the triangle position. Instead of pulling my brother down with my weight, he shoots his hips forward which allows him to remain standing. The more erect his body gets, the better chance he will have to defend and escape. Because I am in tight to his body and have control of his elbow, I decide not to abandon my attack.

5 With my left hand still controlling my brother's elbow, I release my right grip and hook my right arm around the inside of his left leg.

6 Using my hook around my brother's left leg, I pull my body in a counterclockwise direction. This shifts my positioning and puts more of my weight between my brother's legs, making it difficult for him to remain standing, which is his defense for my attack.

7 My brother falls forward because of my new positioning, and I finish with the armlock.

DEALING WITH FLYING ATTACK DEFENSE OPTION #2

1 After jumping up with my flying attack, I have assumed the standard triangle position. I have a left sleeve grip above my brother's right elbow and a right high grip on his collar.

2 Before my falling weight can drag my brother down, he thrusts his hips forward and curls his trapped arm up toward his head. Notice how this lifts my body back up. My brother's defense is strong right now, but I still want to finish with a submission.

3 I release my high grip and plant my right hand above my brother's left knee. I still have my left grip above his elbow. Right now my hips are centered with his body. I will need to reposition my hips off to his right side to make him collapse forward.

4 Posting on my right hand, I arch my hips and straighten my body. This creates a little separation between my hips and my brother's torso, and I'm going to use that separation to shift my hips to his right side.

5 Having shifted my hips to my brother's right, I remove my hand from his right knee. Notice how this swings my body down to my brother's right side. Now I am going to rotate in a counterclockwise direction so that my head comes closer to his right foot.

6 Having rotated so that my head is close to my brother's right foot, the change in my weight causes my brother to drop forward. Notice that I am still controlling his elbow with my left grip.

7 Releasing my sleeve grip, I wrap the crook of my left arm around my brother's right arm and let it slide up to his wrist. At the same time, I begin to throw my left leg over his head. Notice how my leg skims the side of his head to keep everything tight.

8 After throwing my leg over my brother's head, I further rotate my body in a counterclockwise direction to get my hips aligned with his elbow. Once I've done that, I finish the submission by pinning his hand to my chest with my left arm, pinching my knees together, and arching my hips.

DEALING WITH FLYING ATTACK DEFENSE OPTION #3

1 After jumping up with my flying attack, I assume the standard triangle position. I have a left sleeve grip above my brother's right elbow and a right collar grip.

2 As my body comes down to the mat, I instantly become aware that my brother has excellent triangle defense. He has bent his trapped arm up toward his head, and he is locking it in place with his left arm. He is also using his shoulders to resist the pressure of the triangle. Rethinking my game plan, I immediately plant my right hand on the inside of his left leg. Notice that I am not gripping his leg—my fingers are on one side, and my thumb is on the other. I then push off my planted hand to rotate my body in a counterclockwise direction.

3 As I continue to rotate my body in a counterclockwise direction, I maintain my sleeve grip. Because I have kept my legs locked down, my brother still thinks I'm trying to isolate his arm.

4 When I reach the point where I can no longer rotate by pushing with my posted right hand, I abandon my sleeve grip and hook my left hand around the back of my brother's leg to help continue my rotation. Notice that my feet are still hooked above my brother's head—this slows down his escape and allows me to transition to my next position.

5 With my left hand still cupped around the inside of my brother's left leg, I reach my right hand behind my brother's right leg and cup just above his knee. Notice how my feet are still crossed behind my brother's head. I know I have lost the triangle at this point, but I'm trying to buy time by forcing my brother to fight out of it.

6 Losing the triangle, I quickly corkscrew my body in a counterclockwise direction to keep my brother from controlling my legs. As I do this, I use my hands to pull my body between his legs.

7 Having pulled my upper body between my brother's legs, I drop my knees as fast as possible and wedge them between his legs. I also reach my right hand up and grab what I can. Here I am grabbing the bottom of my brother's gi, but if he was lower, I could just as easily latch onto his belt.

8 Pulling on my brother's gi with my right grip, I push on his legs with my knees to drop him down into a squat position.

9 Kicking out my brother's legs with my knees, he comes down on top of me.

10 Continuing to kick out my brother's legs, he comes all the way down on top of me. Notice how his head is slightly lower than mine. You don't want your opponent's head too high or too low. You know you have perfect positioning when you can just see over the top of your opponent's head.

11 As I sit up, I keep my feet hooked underneath my brother's legs. This not only limits his movement, but it will also allow me to follow him if he manages to move.

12 I reach my right arm over his shoulder and latch onto his left collar with my right hand. From here I can continue with the choke or move into a different back attack.

THROW DEFENSE TO FLYING ARMLOCK

Flying attacks are not strictly offensive. In this situation, your opponent isolates one of your arms and steps in to throw. Instead of allowing him to do that, you defend by using the arm he isolated to launch into a flying attack. When done with the right timing and speed, this technique is very effective.

1 My brother and I square off with the same foot forward.

2 My brother obtains a sleeve grip on my right arm, and he reaches his right arm underneath my left arm to establish an under-hook. Here he could be forcing me to stand straight up or trying to execute a koshi-guruma throw.

3 Using his under-hook to stand me straight up, my brother steps in for the throw. The moment I feel his movement, I throw my left hip forward into his hip, which is the standard defense for judo throws. At the same time, I latch onto his collar with my left hand and force my elbow toward the mat. Notice how this locks his right elbow in place without me having to physically grab it. This technique can be applied in a number of situations when you want to trap your opponent's elbow but not alert him to the fact.

4 Still gripping the front of my brother's collar with my right hand and the back of his collar with my left, I use those grips to pull myself into him as I jump. I throw my right leg across the front of his belt, and my left leg heads toward the back of his head.

5 Keeping my right grip on his collar, my weight drops and pulls my brother forward. Notice that I still have my brother's right arm trapped underneath mine, and that I'm sliding my left hand down his arm.

6 As I come down onto my shoulders, I throw my left leg over my brother's head. To finish the submission, I pinch my knees together, arch my hips, and push back on my brother's arm with my left elbow.

FLYING TRIANGLE OFF SINGLE LEG

Although in the previous section we covered several ways to stop an opponent who shoots in for a single leg takedown, the flying triangle is by far my favorite. Your opponent's shot sets you up perfectly for this technique, making it extremely explosive. I've won many competitions with this move. It's by far my most successful flying attack.

1 My brother and I are squared off with opposite feet forward.

2 My brother shoots in for my front leg. Immediately I drop my right hand behind his left elbow to separate his arm from his body and take away his leverage to lift my leg. At the same time, I plant my left hand on the side of his head and push it down toward his right foot.

3 My brother lifts my right leg. With my right hand still controlling his elbow, I straighten my leg so I can put it on the outside of his left leg. On this move you don't want your leg trapped between your opponent's legs.

4 With my right foot hooked around the outside of my brother's left leg, I am set up to establish the triangle position. Now all I have to do is close the distance.

5 Planting my left hand on my brother's back for support, I push off with my left foot and jump into the air.

6 I crash my left leg down between my brother's right shoulder and neck, landing right in the triangle position. Sometimes your opponent will stay in this position, and sometimes he will drop to his knees. Either way, you'll have the triangle position.

7 I come down into the triangle position. With my left hand still controlling my brother's elbow, I drop my right hand down to his sleeve. Notice how my hips are arched to keep my brother from dropping his weight and stacking me.

8 I pull my brother's arm to my left side using my left sleeve grip. My right hand is also controlling his arm, helping to pull it across. Notice that I haven't done anything with my feet at this point.

9 With my brother's arm now on my left side, I reach my right hand up and grab my left shin. From this position, I can put enough pressure on his head with my right elbow to finish the submission.

10 I decide to finish my brother with the traditional submission and throw the crook of my right leg over my left foot. Notice that I still haven't taken my right hand off my shin. With everything locked tight, my brother either taps in submission or goes to sleep.